BETTY & PANSY'S SEVERE QUEER REVIEW OF SAN FRANCISCO

An Irreverent, Opinionated Guide
to the Bars, Clubs, Restaurants,
Cruising Areas, Performing Arts
and other Attractions
of the Queer Mecca

Fifth Edition

By Betty Pearl and Pansy

CLEIS
PRESS

Published in the United States by Cleis Press Inc., P.O. Box 8933, Pittsburgh, Pennsylvania 15221, and P.O. Box 14684, San Francisco, California 94114.

Cover art: Scott Idelmen
Book design: Karen Huff
Logo art: Juana Alicia
Illustrations: Jim Coughenour

Printed in the United States.
Fifth Edition.
10 9 8 7 6 5 4 3 2 1

Library of Congress Cataloging-in-Publication Data

Betty.
    [Betty and Pansy's Severe Queer Review of San Francisco]
    Betty and Pansy's Severe Queer Review of San Francisco: an irreverent, opinionated guide to the bars, clubs, restaurants, cruising areas, performing arts and other attractions of the Queer Mecca/by Betty Pearl and Pansy —5th ed.
    p. cm.
    ISBN: 1-57344-056-6 (paper)
    1. Gay men—Travel—California—San Francisco—Guidebooks. 2. Lesbians—Travel—California—San Francisco—Guidebooks. 3. Gay men—Services for—California—San Francisco—Guidebooks. 4. Lesbians—Services for—California—San Francisco—Guidebooks. 5. Gay communities—California—San Francisco—Guidebooks. 6. Lesbian communities—California—San Francisco—Guidebooks. 7. San Francisco (Calif.)—Guidebooks. I. Pansy. II. Title.
HQ76.3.U52C23   1996
917.94'610453—dc20   96-20411
                             CIP

We would like to dedicate this book
to Jerome Caja.

She was a low-down dirty ho'
and we loved her more than
the Smithsonian could ever imagine.
San Francisco is a mighty
bleak place without
the queen mother of queers.

Acknowledgments

We would like to thank the following people:
Barbie Jesus Exxon Valdez Marilyn Kennedy...Jones,
Cary Boisvert, Dave Ford, Elyse Wolland, Fernando Aguayo
Garcia, Frédérique Delacoste, Gerard Koskovich, John Hayes,
Hunter Long Fox III, Jim Coughenour, Junkyard, Ken White,
Kevin Stark, Laura Thomas, Mabel Maney, Niall Yoshizumi,
Peggy Sue, Raymond Melville, Robert Miotke, Scott O'Hara,
Sian Van Cortlandt, Thor Butkus, Tom Lakritz, and
WedgeMan.

CONTENTS

ABBREVIATIONS

A.K.A.	Also Known As
B&P	Betty and Pansy
B&B	Bed and Breakfast
C&W	Country and Western
DNA	Does Not Apply
G&L	Gay and Lesbian
J/O	Jack-Off
M/F	Male/Female
SF	San Francisco
S/M	Sadomasochism
SOMA	South of Market Street district
SQR	Severe Queer Review
TS	Transsexual
TV	Transvestite
???	We don't know (sorry, we tried!)

WELCOME TO
SAN FRANCISCO

Whether you are a gay tourist, a recent transplant or a local, we believe (deep in our hearts) that this tome of information has something to offer you. Be sure to wear a flower in your hair. Consider us your great and mighty masters of wisdom and knowledge (try and snatch this pebble from our hands).

We began the *Severe Queer Review* because, when we both worked at A Different Light Bookstore, tourists kept asking us for a gay guide to San Francisco, and we had to sit down and plan their week. We spent a year visiting all the queer neighborhood bars and then compiling our results. Unsure of whether the book would sell, we printed only five hundred copies, which sold out in six weeks. The second printing sold out in eight weeks. Four editions later, we had sold about twenty thousand books, including our reviews of New York City and Washington, D.C., before being approached by our new glamorous publisher Cleis. We hope you adore them, because we do. It means a hell of a lot less work for us and a better product for you.

We would love to hear from *some* of you. If you have any advice, complaints, compliments, historical information, or anything you think we should know for future editions, please write to us at Cleis Press, PO Box 8933, Pittsburgh, PA 15221, or e-mail: pghcleis@aol.com.

Love you, mean it.
Betty and Pansy

NEIGHBORHOODS

Bernal Heights
Many home-owning lesbian couples live here. Primarily residential, it is home to an amazingly diverse cross-section of ethnic backgrounds.

Castro
The gay neighborhood. The businesses are queer, the people are queer, the homes are queer, sometimes even the children are queer. Considered by some to be the gay ghetto since you can go days here without bumping into a straight person.

China Basin
Occasionally a club opens on one of the piers in this freezing cold neighborhood. It is rarely worth the trip.

Duboce Triangle
Mostly residential, the neighborhood borders are Duboce, Market and Castro Streets. Queer folks like to live here because it is so centrally located.

Financial District
Besides one gay bar and the fact that tons of queers work here, the area is of little interest.

Glen Park
Home to many lesbians.

The Haight
The upper Haight is home to a bunch of lost hippies, deadheads, homeless teens and gawking tourists. The lower Haight contains the workplaces, homes and hangouts of many queer and straight, downwardly mobile, pierced youngsters. Betty used to and Pansy still does live in the middle.

The Mission
Latino central. The birthplace of the whole city. Fun restaurants, theaters and cafés. Not-so-fun street evangelists, fag bashers and junkies. Best by day, occasionally frightening by night. Home to many poor yet culturally sensitive faggots and dykes. Some folks bet this is where the new queer community will blossom.

Nob Hill

A.k.a. Snob Hill. Home to the richer and more upwardly mobile homosexual and occasionally gay men and women. Wonder how they feel about the Nob Hill Cinema? See Cruising, Theaters, page 98.

Noe Valley

A frightening number of young straight couples live here in their first homes. Their ill-bred and spoiled spawn, known to ride in Aprica carriages, have haircuts that are scarily similar to middle-aged lesbians. Dykes and fags who live here pass with little notice. Many cafés and cute shops. Lots of sun, not much sex.

North Beach

Tourist central. Go for the pasta, City Lights Bookstore, Café Trieste, and to laugh and point at tired old beatniks.

Pacific Heights

A.k.a. Specific Whites. Where the truly rich, established, powerful and self-important of our communities host hundred-dollars-a-plate fundraisers for friends and candidates of their choice. Sniff, sniff. Do you smell Uncle Tom's Log Cabin Club? If you feel the need to make love by firelight near a grand piano while the lover is away, then, um, become a houseboy here.

Polk

Eek. Before the Castro was reinvented as queer central in the sixties and seventies, this was the center of it all. Some folks are still waiting for the others to return. Most have decided to park it at the bar and drink until the others return. Home to boy hookers, washed-up drunks and prowling closet cases. Pansy first found gainful employment in SF here. Betty and Pansy discovered Ben-Hur (R.I.P.) and the wonders of video booths here.

Potrero Hill

Some gay folks who want cheaper rent, larger amounts of space and a less dangerous place than SOMA choose this as an alternative. Where they filmed *Pacific Heights*. O.J. Simpson also happens to be from here.

SOMA

Home to artists, the rich but adventurous, leather freaks who never want to leave and folks who want to stretch their rent dollar. Many gay bars and lurky hangouts (inside and outside) can be found here.

Tenderloin

Eek. Double Eek. What is known in most cities as the Red Light District. Hookers, pimps, junkies, and Betty and Pansy with tear gas at the ready trying to review queer bars. Not as scary as some think, but we wouldn't want to visit on a regular basis.

Twin Peaks

Home to Queens and a few Lesbians and Straight Folk who want a good view of the sunrise. They must also enjoy fog and extremely curvy streets.

Note: While visiting San Francisco, you will also encounter references to a number of neighborhoods that rarely interest queer people: Chinatown, Crocker Amazon, Diamond Heights, Excelsior, The Fillmore, Hunter's Point, Ingleside, Japantown, Laurel Heights, Marina, Parkside, Presidio, Richmond, St. Francis Woods, Sunset, Visitacion Valley, West Portal, and Western Addition.

TRANSPORTATION

If you are not traveling by car, we suggest you call MUNI at (415) 673-MUNI (673-6864) and ask about the many options available. A Fast Pass is $38.00 and good for the whole month; a Weekly Pass is $9.00, and a Day Pass is $2.25. These passes let you ride MUNI buses, trains and cable cars. The Fast Pass also allows you to ride BART and CalTrans within San Francisco. At a dollar a crack for a bus or train ride, or three dollars a crack for a cable car ride, the passes are well worth the expense.

Even if you don't plan to take public transit, buy a San Francisco street and transit map. You can get one at most corner stores as well as A Different Light Bookstore. It includes a wealth of information such as MUNI subway and bus lines and is indispensable in helping you find your way around town. For just over two dollars, it is the best bargain in all of SF.

Other options include walking, which is nice in most places but not wise at night in some neighborhoods (as previously noted. If you are at a bar or club, the staff will gladly call a cab for you. It is generally easy to flag one down while in SOMA, the Polk or the Castro. In other neighborhoods, you probably need to call. See Phone Numbers, page 146.

NEWSPAPERS

Check out the following publications for current local happenings.

Bay Area Reporter (B.A.R.)

The middle-of-the-road alternative gay rag. Most pick it up to check the obits to see if anyone they know has made their final transition to that disco in the sky. Also, it has the most massage (euphemism for hookers) ads of any of the papers. It is free, published weekly and arrives on Thursday mornings.

Bay Guardian

Hip, young, politically active journalists who give a damn. Probably has the only investigative reporting in the city with the exception of the *SF Weekly*. Cartoonist Tom Tomorrow and the "Ask Isadora" sex-advice column by Isadora Alman are the best parts. A free weekly paper that comes out on Wednesday.

Bay Times

The best queer alternative paper. Includes the most stuff for women. The *Bay Times* has the best calendar of events. The best columnist is Nan Parks, who does outreach from the straight community. We love Nan. It is free, published every other week and arrives on Thursday evenings.

The Chronicle

Founded in the mid-nineteenth century as a sleazy gossip tabloid for the theater district, the *Chron* has grown into the Bay Area's major daily newspaper/litter-liner without changing its original journalistic principles much at all. Coverage of queer issues is adequate but the tone sometimes makes you wonder if the publishers ever come into the city from the clueless upscale suburbs where they reside.

The Examiner

A Randolph Hearst production. Poor Tanya. From rifle-wielding militant to white pumps after Labor Day. Enough said. Actually, *The Examiner* is one of the last of its breed, an afternoon daily. The staff includes openly—for that matter flamingly—queer critics Barry Walters (rock) and David Bonetti (art). Look to their reviews for the latest on big-time dyke and homo artists and performers in town.

Frontiers

The newest gay rag in town, *Frontiers* is the SF edition of the L.A. publication, with which it frequently shares feature stories. The writing and production values are slick, and the editorial politics generally moderate. *Frontiers* has the most acidulous gossip column in town, with something bitter to say about just about everyone. Published twice a month.

The Independent

This rag is published by the conservative semi-, sort of openly, you-know-what scion of a right wing dynasty. *The Independent* helped launch former top cop, former mayor, Frank Jordan—a mealy-mouthed crypto-Republican puppet of the Chamber of Commerce—into the mayor's office. A glorified advertiser that arrives for free three times a week.

Oblivion

A bi-weekly free gay ad rag that has loads of helpful information. The highlight is Joan Jett Blakk's column. The bummer is that they are an obvious Betty & Pansy knock-off.

Odyssey

A gay ad rag at its best. This is great for discovering current and popular bars and clubs for queers in the "Jet Boy" and "Jet Girl" sections. Billy Masters' gossip column rules. It is free and is published every other week.

SF Weekly

The best thing in the whole world is "Real Astrology for an Unreal World" by Rob Brezsny. This dude knows our every waking step (and our sleeping ones, too). The other fun feature is Dan Savage's sex-advice column, "Savage Love" a.k.a. "Hey, Faggot." *SF Weekly* has great politics, too. It is free and published weekly on Wednesdays.

Jesus Wants Me
for a
Jim Beam

Our definitions of bars and clubs
might be different from yours.
Listed here by neighborhood
are seven-night-a-week spots.
Establishments that are open
less than daily are located in
the Clubs chapter. Some of
these bars do have dance floors
and DJs. If it is not mentioned, it
is safe to assume that a dance
floor does not exist. There is
also no cover charge unless
otherwise noted. Though it is
sad to say, gay bars are still
closing left and right. Please
call in advance to see if it is
open and at the same location.

CASTRO

See Maps, page 160.

Badlands

4121 18th St. at Castro. Phone: (415) 626-9320.
Hours: Mon thru Fri open at 11:30 a.m., Sat and Sun 11 a.m. to 2 a.m. M/F: 99/1.

Thursday nights pump our 'nads. Retro music and retro men make a beautiful combo. Badlands has a C&W theme with bad skylights and the most exciting collection of license plates from around the queer world (i.e. *R U 1 2*). We have a couple of favorite staff members—Brian and Malcolm. They really like it when you give them a hard time (or a blowjob). Badlands has a row of pinball machines with crazed queens flipping the flippers faster than they can chug-a-lug their recently mixed Cocksuckers. There are two bathrooms. One is private. The other has two trough urinals, chalkboards and two doors with windows. Despite the high risk of exposure and possible permanent scarlet T (tearoom troll) label, much peek-a-boo takes place. Dancing is strictly forbidden, though Betty challenges this rule as often as possible and has never been reprimanded. There are two pool tables where the aficionados pretend every game is the final match at the nationals where they will dethrone Minnesota Fats. Badlands is one of Betty and Pansy's favorite hangouts.

The Café

2367 Market near Castro and 17th St. Phone: (415) 861-3846.
Hours: weekdays 2 p.m. to 2 a.m., weekends noon to 2 a.m. M/F: 70/30.

The Café, formerly Café San Marcos, was once the only women's bar in the Castro. Though there is still a considerable crowd of women, it is now predominately filled with men and very young folks from the suburbs. It is one of two places to dance in the Castro (the other being the Phoenix). On weekends there is a line down the block. Though the music leaves something to be desired, the DJ generally packs the tiny dance floor, and folks seem to enjoy the music immensely. The Café is a great place to have a drink during the day due to the abundance of windows, the charming little deck and the balcony facing Market Street. The balcony offers a great opportunity for watching, cat-calling, or cruising the passing parade of pedestrians. There are several pinball machines and two pool tables that are always occupied. There is a larger percentage of women during the days and week nights. On Monday nights, bottled domestic beer is $1.25.

Castro Country Club

4058 18th St. at Hartford. Phone: (415) 552-6102.
Hours: Mon thru Fri 2 p.m. to midnight, Sat and Sun 10 a.m. to midnight.
Cover: $1.00, lasts all day. M/F: 80/20.

The sheer number of people in recovery in San Francisco is quite astounding—indeed, the folks marching under the banner of "Living Sober" comprise the single largest contingent in our annual Lesbian, Gay, Bisexual, Transgender Freedom Day Parade—or whatever the hell they're calling it this year. Nowhere in the city's clean-and-sober community is that diversity better represented than at the Castro Country Club. Located within "yoo-hoo" distance of the queer epicenter (corner of Castro and 18th Streets), the club is a welcome change for both the casual visitor and the local Castro denizen alike who yearn for the occasional break from the booze-fueled nights that many associate with our neck of the hood. Quite friendly and very animated, the atmosphere is certainly not the maudlin, smoke-filled stereotype that so many associate with establishments of this kind.

The club, a converted Victorian house, which has been lovingly and painstakenly renovated by the owner of the building, is divided into several sections, creating an environment suitable to just about every mood. The main sitting room has more than a few cozy tables and a large overstuffed couch where one can just sit and hang out or, if need be, discuss your existential angst-ridden life with your sister/friend/lover/ex-lover. Adjacent to the sitting room is the bar, which is usually the main convergence point in the club, featuring coffee, lattés, soft drinks, bottled water and any of a number of things to eat. Towards the back of the club, there is another smaller sitting room that sometimes doubles as a game room—though it is doubtful whether anyone has played board games back there in years. Adjacent to this other sitting room is the "theater" where a small elevated platform holds several rows of seats removed from a real movie theater. A large screen television recessed in one of the walls plays the latest videos nightly. If sitting indoors doesn't work, you can check out the backyard patio where, during the summer, one can sit and relax and take in the sun. The front steps are legendary on sunny weekend days. Sober queens fill the steps and let the comments rip no matter who is walking by. Daily "dues" are usually a dollar.

Castro Station

456B Castro bet. Market and 18th St. Phone: (415) 626-7220.
Hours: 6 a.m. to 2 a.m. M/F: 99/1.

Please do not confuse this bar with the MUNI stop half a block away, though many do. The musical selections here curl our hair better than hot rollers. There are pinball machines, computer games and one pool table. The bathroom on the left is highly cruisy. The bathroom on right is for privacy. Betty was once shocked to spot a male centerfold from the pages of *Advocate Men* at this establishment. He had been dubbed a "hot man with a lot of well-deserved attitude." What the hell was he doing playing pool at the Castro Station, for Christ's sakes? You can observe the crowd from the other side of street, which is often the preferable choice.

Daddy's

440 Castro bet. Market and 18th St. Phone: (415) 621-8732.
Hours: 6 a.m. to 2 a.m. M/F: 99/1.

Daddy's inhabits the space that was once a gay bar known as The Bear. Daddy's staff ripped everything up and out and started from scratch. The interior is much nicer than the old bar. Of course, we had to ask if they ever figured out why The Bear had a strange and lingering stench. It appears that when they ripped up the floor they discovered three carcasses. They might have been cats but were unidentifiable. There is a bar in the front and one in the back. Unfortunately, the wonderful back deck is no longer accessible to patrons. The bathrooms are still in disrepair but the staff has plans to remodel them. It appears the city won't let them put in a urinal for some bizarre inexplicable reason. So there will be no future tearooms at this watering hole. Both of us ran into folks that we knew well (and liked), which to our minds is always a good sign. The place was hot and lively and the bartenders and barbacks were cute and friendly. These guys are big on football games. The pinball machines are hot. There is a DJ seven days a week but no dancing.

Detour

2348 Market bet. Castro and Noe. Phone: (415) 861-6053.
Hours: 2 p.m. to 2 a.m. M/F: 95/5.

The Detour is a small, dark and crowded bar. It is known for its cruisy good-looking crowd of young men that thrives on attitude, sexual tension and the loud, hip musical selections. When you are a slut who drinks like a fish, every moment and dollar counts. Beer at the Detour is cheap and the patrons are cheaper. On Sundays, bottled domestic beer is $1.00 until 10 p.m. They do play the best music in the Castro, and some would say the city. The Detour is also known for its attractive staff, although most of the friendly faces and attitudes have disappeared. The pool table and pin-ball machines are always busy. The bathroom is highly cruisy and there is often much hedging for a better position and view. The two oddly angled trough urinals and conveniently located mirrors make for an interesting tearoom experience. If you would like privacy, ask the bartender for the key, which is attached to a giant boot. Our only true objection is the perpetually annoying subliminal laser neon sign. The proliferation of these devices must be stopped, at any cost.

The Edge

4149 18th St. at Collingwood. Phone: (415) 863-4027.
Hours: noon to 2 a.m. M/F: 100/0.

The Edge is a standard Castro clone bar. The interior, the service, the crowd, the music, well, every aspect of The Edge is merely passable. We have no complaints nor any real compliments. The highlight of an Edge experience seems to be the pinball. Many of the thirty- to fifty-year-old gentlemen seem to be visiting this establishment solo. Conversations range from hushed to non-existent. As we sat at the bar trying to squeeze blood from a turnip, we realized that we finally missed Francine's. Remember, Francine's? It was that dyke bar of yesteryear located at the address The Edge now inhabits. Scary truck drivers and rugby players and bulldaggers of all varieties used to play pool here and have truly frightening arguments highlighted by the occasional fistfight. We always ducked or crossed the street when passing Francine's, unsure if a chair might fly through the plate glass window at any given moment. In the wake of Francine's absence, The Edge has opted for a more peaceful yet brooding atmosphere. Domestic beers are $1.00 all day on Mondays. On Wednesdays, house cocktails are $1.50 from 9 p.m. to 1 a.m. On Sundays, draft beers are $ .50 from 4 to 10 p.m.

Harvey's

500 Castro at 18th St. Phone: (415) 431-HARV. Hours: DNA. M/F: DNA.

We must give you the dish sight unseen since, at the time of this writing, Harvey's is on the verge of opening. Our first problem would be the tire tracks across the back of The Elephant Walk bar that inhabited this space for more than twenty years. The landlord seemed not the least bit concerned with the historical significance of The Elephant Walk to the gay and lesbian community. After the White Night Riots in 1979, police stormed The Elephant Walk, dragged out fags and beat them; the bar sued the city's ass and won. For years The Elephant Walk had to put up with the impending loss of their lease but bounced back time and time again. Now we are being told that Harvey's (named after Harvey Milk who is probably spinning in his grave) is going to be a gay Hard Rock Café. Plans hint at a gay sports bar and restaurant with gay sports memorabilia (i.e. Martina's racket, Greg's speedo, etc.) It sounds like a feasible and harmless enough idea but why must it replace what was a cornerstone of the queer community in San Francisco?

The Men's Room

3988 18th St. at Noe. Phone: (415) 861-1310.
Hours: noon to 2 a.m. M/F: 90/10.

The bartenders are courteous and friendly. The patrons all seem to know one another and like to drink and watch movies on the two televisions. The cat that lives here performs such wonderful treats as licking her butt and then your cocktail, or going helter-skelter knocking over drinks and ashtrays on her way to or from the litter box. On one visit, Betty was recounting some nightmarish drama in her life to Pansy when the door opened and the entire crowd fell silent. Two frightening queens strolled in. The thinner of the two, who was dressed in a quasi-uniform, raced to the end of the bar and started chatting with a friend. The other looked like Humpty Dumpty with male pattern baldness and a bad perm. Humpty was drunk as a skunk and was trying to follow her friend's path. Ms. Dumpty was lurching from side to side knocking down innocent people in a random path of destruction. Of course both Betty and Pansy were trapped in her line of fire. We prayed she would fall and pass out but, as we all know, weebles wobble but they don't fall down.

The Metro

3600 16th St. at Noe and Market. Phone: (415) 703-9750.
Hours: 2:30 p.m. to 2 a.m.; open at 1 p.m. on weekends. M/F: 60/40.

This place has balconies that face the rather large intersection of Market, Noe and 16th. For years the balconies remained unpeopled. Then one day, some drag queen must have used a hairpin to pick the lock on the sliding glass doors, releasing hordes of cat-calling, brew-swillin' know-nothings. Our community has suffered immeasurably ever since. Ladies, keep your hat pins to yourself. The interior is a morass of neon, black furniture, and chatty drinking folks. Betty was assaulted recently by the sight of acid-wash. Her waitron, who would rather die than crack a smile, had obviously not heard that acid wash was universally deemed unacceptable over ten years ago. A recent upswing in business can probably be blamed on the addition of karaoke. Our source informs us that Tuesday nights are karaoke night and The Metro is packed. The patrons seem to take themselves quite seriously. Our opulent superstar source informs us that she has never before heard such a heartfelt rendition of "I've Never Been To Me." If you work downtown, travel in packs of threes or fours, swill cocktails, are serious about karaoke, and enjoy John Grisham novels, this is the place for you. When the restaurant is open, they accept credit cards.

Midnight Sun

4067 18th St. at Castro. Phone: (415) 861-4186.
Hours: noon to 2 a.m. M/F: 98/2.

A.k.a. Midnight Scum and/or Midnight Slum. This is the only gay video bar that we know of in San Francisco. Wednesday night, they play classic videos from the sixties, seventies and eighties. Saturday night, they play comedy videos from 7 to 10 p.m. It has become a sanctuary for the endangered species known as sweater queens. The popularity of this spot never seems to wane. There is often a line to get in. This line of folks is particularly fun to harass. The videos have been elevated from a pretext to visit to the only real reason to visit. The management now posts signs outside the bar announcing the screening times for shows like *Gypsy* or *Barbra* on

HBO. The comedy clips are more fun than the music. A tepid cruisiness pervades the crowd. Thank god, the bartenders are more brave, aggressive and willing.

Moby Dick

4049 18th St. at Hartford. Phone: DNA. Hours: noon to 2 a.m. M/F: 90/10.

A.k.a. Moldy Dick. A men's bar (Moby DICK—get it?) but women like it also. The pool table is hardly competitive, the pinball machines are always available, and there are never any fights, which is kind of a shame. Often there are some very drunken thirty-something locals here, so if you need a place to sleep and cannot deal with the Detour, work this bar. The atmosphere at Moby Dick is often mellow to the extreme despite the hi-energy multi-video screens. They do need to stop hosting such horrible rotating art exhibits. After a few of their delicious slushy drink specials, you probably will not even notice the bad male nudes. Plus they have an incredible fish tank running the whole length of the bar. Some folks have complained of getting headaches after spending a Sunday afternoon at Moby Dick. Probably because they are sucking down the blended drink specials a wee too quickly. On Sunday, they serve two-for-one Sex on the Beach out of the slurpy machine. During the week, this bar has a two-for-one Margarita happy hour. If it comes out of a slurpy machine—you cannot go wrong. This is one of the favorite pinball hangouts of the Pinochle Palace and cutting edge queer theater set. It is also the official bar of the Hot 'n' Hunky staff. The staff is just wonderful and always willing to make change for the pinball machine. There are two bathrooms. The one downstairs is pregnant with tearoom potential but despite Betty's many attempts, no fish are biting.

The Pendulum

4146 18th St. at Collingwood. Phone: (415) 863-4441.
Hours: 7 a.m. to 2 a.m. M/F: 98/2.

Ever since the loss of Eagle Creek, this is the only gay bar in San Francisco that has a predominantly black clientele. The Pendulum hosts well-attended and exuberant parties. The weekends are packed and everyone is having fun. The staff is friendly and quick. The pool table is always busy. Once we spotted an author of one of those how-I-survived-AIDS-by-eating-nuts-and-berries-and-touching-my-inner-child-in-a-special-way books. He wrote it with his lover who Pansy noted is "now foraging in that great forest in the sky." Who is in charge of false advertising for AIDS self-help books anyway?

Phoenix

482 Castro at 18th St. Phone: (415) 552-6827.
Hours: 1 p.m. to 2 a.m. M/F: 95/5.

The Phoenix is a Castro institution. Betty and Pansy, however, do not want to be institutionalized. The Phoenix wins the award for having the youngest crowd of any gay bar in SF. The atmosphere is loud, crowded and sweaty on weekends. The crowd is very racially mixed—Asian, Latin and black, with older white chickenhawks thrown in for sport. Best times to visit are weekend nights. In the evenings folks like to dance here but the dance floor is small and usually quite packed. One of Betty's friends got his wallet pickpocketed here. On another visit Betty witnessed the bartender scream "Pickpocket!" point at a female patron and sail across the bar to bust her. Though the staff is vigilant, it is a good idea to keep a close eye on your wallet. The sidewalk sale after the bar closes is a nightmare of gargantuan proportions, best described as a paddle oven of verbal taunts from tipsy, snipey, jaded, barely post-pubescent bitches.

Twin Peaks

401 Castro at Market and 17th St. Phone: (415) 864-9470.
Hours: Noon to 2 a.m. M/F: 98/2.

A.k.a. The Glass Coffin, God's Waiting Room, and Tomb with a View. The horribly rude nicknames are derived from two characteristics: the two walls of windows at street level and the senior crowd always in attendance. Twin Peaks was the first gay bar in Amerikkka with windows at street level. The staff is excellent. The laid back, quiet crowd has friendly conversations with each other and occasionally plays cards. Twin Peaks is busy night and day. The lovely interior includes an antique bar that is an excellent piece of woodwork. The balcony is one of Betty and Pansy's favorite hiding spots. It is a great place to have a quiet drink and conversation with a friend if you do not want to be interrupted or seen by folks you know. The music is retro and we love it. The main drawback of Twin Peaks is that they do not serve bottled beer. There are individual tables and comfy chairs, but sometimes it is so busy you have to stand. Two thumbs up.

Uncle Bert's Place

4086 18th St. at Castro. Phone: (415) 431-8616.
Hours: 6 a.m. to 2 a.m. M/F: 65/35.

The regulars' attire generally consists of sweatshirts, jeans and other casual duds. You can tell these people watch sports (on TV and off). The back deck is very nice and they have barbecues on a regular basis. If there is a Forty-Niners' game, the back deck is packed. A historical point of interest: one of Betty's clean and sober friends bottomed out here. At the time, he was a closeted straight boy visiting the Castro during Halloween (a practice that must be stopped immediately). He got "separated" from his friends and made his way into this gay bar. At one point he awoke from a blackout on the pool table. Keep in mind that he was dressed as a beaten Amish child. A later blackout landed him on the floor of the bathroom. He was scooped up by a male nurse and taken to the nurse's apartment. This health care professional was not very professional as he brought Betty's friend "out" in the old-fashioned sense of the word.

Staff here have been known to be *extremely* rude to customers to get them to leave before closing time, including turning off a friend's pinball game, even though it was on the last ball, and actually hanging up the pay phone while someone was in the middle of a conversation. All to get people out by 1:45! We can only hope the bartender in question had a hot date waiting. Uncle Bert's windows face 18th Street and the folks that sit here are the cruisiest Lurky Turkeys you have ever seen. Do not accidentally nod your head or they will probably follow you home.

M I S S I O N

See Maps, page 176.

Dalva's

3121 16th St. at Valencia. Phone: (415) 252-7740.
Hours: 4 p.m. to 2 a.m. (open at 2 p.m. on Fridays). M/F: 50/50.

This is not necessarily a gay bar, per se, but many gay people hang out here. If you like to drink, know your liquor and like your hootch in good solid glassware, this is the spot. They know how to pour a pint of Guinness, have Knockando Scotch (which is hard to find), and the house drink is the Cosmopolitan made by Michelle. This is a perfect spot to hang out with friends before or after dinner and a smart choice for a third date. There is a noticeable lack of attitude and a plethora of great music. No pinball, no pool and no computer games. DJ on Tuesday thru Thursday, and Saturday.

El Rio

3158 Mission at Army. Phone: (415) 282-3325.
Hours: 3 p.m. to 2 a.m., Sun and Mon close at midnight. M/F: 50/50.

Known as "The Best Dive in San Francisco," El Rio features evenings of free pool, oyster feeds, rock 'n' roll, and salsa/Brazilian music. The crowd here has recently been infused with too many straight and non-Latino people. It is still very popular. In fact, allegedly, the fire marshal busted this place for being too packed. Now one can look forward to lines outside. Fierce parties are often held on Thursday night by community-based organizations (i.e. GELAAM). This is also the best pick-up spot for the hottest Latina lesbians. El Rio reminds us of that certain straight bar back home that gay people could go to and feel comfortable.

The spacious setting has a large bar area with a pool table, and a gorgeous backyard with lots of plants, an outside heater and a huge cut-out of Carmen Miranda. You can gain entrance to the dance floor on the other side of the bar near the back by the pool table. This is a great place to hang out with friends, especially on Sunday afternoons. Sometimes it is appropriated by queer punk bands in an effort to do their own shows. Be on the lookout for posters in the Mission. Occasionally the cover here can be as high as $7.00 so call to check it out and to see whether it is a particularly queer evening.

Esta Noche

3079 16th St. at Valencia. Phone: (415) 861-5757.
Hours: Mon thru Thurs 1 p.m. to 2 a.m., Fri thru Sun 1 p.m. to 3 a.m. M/F: 99/1.

In the seventies, Esta Noche was a very important Chicano queer space. History, however, has not passed it by. It still has serious value for young queers of color. The crowd that populates Esta Noche is very young and most know each other. Remember that bar you and your friends visited religiously when you first came out? It was where you got all your gossip, dates, friends and enemies. Esta Noche is the Latino version. This small bar is drag queen friendly and about seventy-five percent Latino, twenty-five percent other. The DJ music is mostly salsa or disco. The pool table has been pushed aside to make room on the dance floor. A regular told Betty to warn forty-year-old gay white men in polo shirts that "two beers does not make you attractive or give you the ability to dance salsa."

Our friend Raylene has been spotted here inhaling Goldschlager. Her best girlfriend Francine believes that Raylene's intestines are by now surely lined with twenty-four-karat gold as a result. Raylene and Francine, well-known drunken whores, had a bit of a falling out here. Raylene claims that they were having a friendly discussion at the bar when she turned to find Francine in a lip lock of gargantuan proportions with a strange studly Latino hunk. Francine quickly introduced her trick du jour as Manuel. Raylene realized that it must be same Manuel who had picked Francine up at Bahia Cabana on another drunken evening months before. Our Francine got fucked in the alley so hard on that fateful but obviously not educational evening that brick imprints remained on her face for two days afterwards. Raylene, being well-bred, tried to inform Francine, who is Maine White Trash, that one does not kiss strange men in bars even if they have used their dick like a log splitter on your ass. Francine felt that Raylene viciously prevented Francine's return to that brick wall out of nothing more than pure jealousy. Esta Noche often hosts drag shows and has a cover on certain nights. Call to confirm special events, after hours, and possible cover.

La India Bonita

3089 16th St. at Valencia. Phone: (415) 621-9294.
Hours: noon to 2 a.m. M/F: 95/5.

La India Bonita hosts drag shows in Spanish and the audience is respectfully quiet while the queens perform. The crowd also cheers and claps when the performers finish their numbers. Most of the crowd is well acquainted with one another as this is a very familial atmosphere. The men's bathroom is a mess: no lock, broken window, and exposed throne. We highly recommend this place but you have to know how to order drinks in *español.*

Our first visit to this bar was a fun experience. We thought we had crashed a Latino wedding or something. Grandpa was tending bar. Grandma was collecting empties and pushing a mop around. The young drag queens that were racing around could have been the cousins. The best time to visit is during show times, which are followed by dancing. A source informs us that La India Bonita is the best place in the whole Mission on Friday and Saturday nights during shows. He warns white interlopers to behave and not to hit on the straight Mexican guys even though some do want to get their dicks sucked. Don't get caught in the middle of any of the drag-queen feuds. The Sunday strip show is not worth the bother and the dancing during the week is lame. It is all about Friday and Saturday nights. There is often a cover during drag shows and weekend evenings. Call to confirm.

Phonebooth

1398 South Van Ness at 25th St. Phone: (415) 648-4683.
Hours: 10 a.m. to 2 a.m. M/F: 50/50 (men/women and gay/straight).

This is the only gay bar in the Mission that does not have a predominantly Latino crowd. We did not enjoy our first visit much but enjoyed ourselves immensely the second time. The barkeep is always helpful and friendly. This small bar has a pool table, and seating at the bar as well as individual tables. We have been informed by Hunter ("your neighbor girl") that there is an autographed photo of Tom Selleck over the bar. The bartender swears that Tom, who drops in occasionally, is a dear friend of the owner. Whether this is a bizarre marketing strategy or one of those surreal moments in queer history, we are not sure. Hunter's friend Brian wooed patrons here with his tattoos. They were more blown away by his pierced dick, which he exhibited after the patrons chipped in forty dollars to see it.

P O L K

See Maps, page 168.

The Cinch Saloon

1723 Polk at Clay. Phone: (415) 776-4162. Hours: 6 a.m. to 2 a.m. M/F: 90/10.

The Cinch is decorated with a C&W motif, though that motif does not continue in its music or patrons' attire. Scott from Hot 'n' Hunky (see Cafés & Restaurants, page 70) swears that The Cinch makes the best Long Island iced teas in the entire city. Betty finally tried one and one is all you need. It was served in a mason jar. The Cinch's Long Island Iced Tea has officially replaced The Polk Street Punch as the most kickass cocktail on Polk Street. On Betty's last visit, she brought along Laura and Kevin. We got drunk while chatting in the gorgeous backyard. Kevin got cruised in the bathroom. The mirror over the urinal is tilted for a reason, you know. There are pinball and computer games and pool. We played a couple of the pinball machines until after last call and were politely thrown out by staff. Afterwards we stopped at the donut shop on that block and had the best glazed donuts in SF. We bumped into Doug and Chris who were working the sidewalk sale outside of the N' Touch. Betty was much more interested in the yummy donuts and ran back for seconds.

The Gangway

841 Larkin at Geary. Phone: (415) 885-4441.
Hours: 6 a.m. to 2 a.m. M/F: 100/0.

The outside of this bar is scarier than the cozy interior. The first time we visited, Betty had to force Pansy to step over a person lying in the doorway to enter. The interior sports a nautical theme throughout (The Gangway—get it?). The musical selections were very good oldies: Dixie, jazz, disco and a lot of Louis Armstrong. The crowd consisted of half a dozen guys who ranged from thirty year olds to senior citizens. The bartender was an older, friendly gentleman (says he has been there forever). The Gangway ranks as the granddaddy of gay bars in SF as it has been open somewhere over twenty-five years according to the bar-keep. The restrooms were clean and not for cruising. On our second trip, we noticed they had added a pool table, some better lighting and had fixed up the back area a bit. B&P played a few games of pool as there was no one to witness our abysmal pool-playing skills. Pinball machines and computer games are available as well. When we left the bartender said, "Good night, kids," (and we have over seventy years between us).

The Giraffe

1131 Polk at Post. Phone: (415) 474-1702.
Hours: 11:30 a.m. to 2 a.m. M/F: 90/10.

The Giraffe has a dance floor, hardwood floors and lots of seating. This bar used to be quite famous as the home of the upper echelon of Polk Street hustlers. We have noticed that a lot more straight people and even a few yuppy types are hanging out here lately. Bartenders are well-dressed, tidy and very friendly. However, one of the bartenders cornered our friend Raylene as she innocently visited the ladies' room. This brute manhandled our little delicate Raylene and demanded her phone number. (Raylene would probably not be so bitter about this particular incident if he had ever followed up with a call.) Francine, however, is willing to testify on a Bible in a court of law to the contrary. She says that Raylene develops nasty, obsessive crushes on each new bartender at The Giraffe. Raylene admits to having visions of rimming them for hours at a time. She even shamelessly follows them to the bathroom in hopes of making that special "love connection" come true. Francine is not an O.J. juror and so is willing to stand and say, "Raylene is the guilty one." Stop blaming the victims, Raylene. Francine and Raylene, well-known Giraffe patrons, have theorized that perhaps the bartenders might make themselves available for an evening of pleasure at the right price, though there is not a shred of evidence to prove this, and both are too timid and poor to even broach the subject.

There are pinball machines, computer games and a pool table. The carnivalesque-name tie-in touches to the interior are hardly noticeable. Everyone is very talkative and having fun. Bathrooms are somewhat cruisy but nothing ever happens. Presently listed with information as a "video lounge."

Kimos

1351 Polk at Pine. Phone: (415) 885-4535.
Hours: 9 a.m. to 2 a.m. M/F: 90/10.

Kimos is a Hawaiian word that means imperial and royal palace. It is neither. It is, however, a small depressing bar at street level and a much larger bar upstairs with a stage for shows. The bar downstairs is not much fun. The upstairs used to be open only on rare occasion. Well, things are picking up at Kimos. They are now hosting more shows upstairs, where it appears there has been some redecorating, with the possible addition of some neon lights. Whoa, take it easy. Kimos also seems to be going country. Scared of that. They have been hosting ho-downs, potluck barbecues, country music on certain nights of the week and drink specials for those in cowboy or cowgirl attire. Other happenings include: Forty-Niner games on a big screen television, a buns contest during full moon, dance theater performances, and the infamous drag shows every Friday at 10 p.m. Kimos' motto is "Cocktails and Friends Meet at Kimos."

The Motherlode

1002 Post at Larkin. Phone: (415) 928-6006.
Hours: 6 a.m. to 2 a.m. M/F: a constant source of speculation.

Motherlode likes to think of itself as "The Home of the Real Queens of San Francisco." In the evenings the music is loud, the bar is smoky and crowded, and there is rarely any place to sit. This place seems like a straight disco with a lot of single women at first glimpse. Look closer. Many—probably all—of those women are actually drag queens, transvestites, and pre- and post-op transsexuals. There is an equally large number of male folks (both straight and gay) who are grooving on their booties. The staff is extremely aggressive and asks male patrons to leave if they're not ordering drinks. The crowd inside and outside is pretty tough. Pansy was harassed on the sidewalk by passing motorists. There is a horseshoe-shaped bar that fills about one third of the small space. There have been rumors circulating for years that they are moving to a larger space. They seriously considered one location further up Polk Street but the church next door had a cow. Shows on Friday and Saturday at 11:00 alternate between drag and strip as well as benefits. Best time to visit is Tuesday through Saturday after 9:30 p.m. There is a sign posted over the front door that states no cameras or videos are allowed. The last time we passed by, some dude was scraping the seasonal window decorations off. He must have been doing lines of the purer stuff because he was scraping like a mad dog, fixing his hair, sniffing and then repeating the process at high speed.

N' Touch

1548 Polk at Sacramento. Phone: (415) 441-8413.
Hours: 2 p.m. to 2 a.m. M/F: 99/1.

This is a bar for queer Asian men and their chickenhawk admirers. Speaking of which, one Francine Lumbert, of the Jackman Lumberts, is a notorious regular here. She is still fuming over our last review, which described her frightening drunken interpretive dance techniques. Since that review, she refuses to set foot on the dance floor except when she slinks across to make use of the bathroom, which is only cruisy when Francine is present. On a recent visit with her friend and conscience, Raylene, they shared a special and rare moment. For a whole hour, at least, there was not one man there that Francine had defiled or deflowered. When Pansy visited with Francine (see, she's here a lot) they spotted a scary Asian Elvis Impersonator. He danced exactly like John Travolta in *Saturday Night Fever.* One of the bartenders fingered Pansy as the very one who helps spew this filth despite her elaborate disguise. Dance floor is equipped with disco balls and gets pretty crowded. The atmosphere is highly cruisy. Though most white guys who visit here are looking for Asian Men, Ms. Pansy was undressed by the lustful gaze of two white dudes. Go figure. There was a bit of controversy regarding some alleged illegal video poker gambling in the back of this establishment. A co-worker informed us that several of his friends had made some cash working those machines. In fact, the bar closed for several months under mysterious circumstances. So if you are visiting, don't rule out a raid. There is a minimal cover on weekends and during special events like the male strip shows they often host. Call the number listed above for cover charge, dates and times.

Old Rick's Gold Lounge

939 Geary at Larkin. Phone: (415) 441-9211.
Hours: 6 a.m. to 2 a.m. M/F: 100/0.

This place truly scares the living bejesus out of us, time and time, again. Every time we arrive, all two to four people freeze and stare at us as if Martians were landing at the front door. The customers are generally older and seem to know one another well. Sometimes customers are sleeping, having slurred chats or are sitting by themselves, but having long conversations anyway. The art is bad and the antiques are faux. On our first visit, we asked for our cokes with no ice (as we are very European) and the barkeep switched to smaller glasses. When we paid with a ten, he rubbed it to see if it was counterfeit. On our second visit, an extremely drunk young dyke from another country stopped to ask us a question before stumbling out. It took us a while to realize that she was speaking English and that she was trying to ask us if we were in love. We laughed and pantomimed "just good friends." This upset her quite a bit and she decided that we needed to be in love with one another. We fled. Our friend Fernando visited years ago. He was wearing five very small simple hoop earrings. Old Rick (who is a big Old Queen) turned to Fernando and said, "I don't like it when men wear earrings, it looks so fruity." Hello? You own a gay bar, queen. Old Rick's does have an Eye-Opener Special from 6 a.m. to 10 a.m., perhaps, Old Rick should attend.

The Polk Gulch Saloon

1100 Polk at Post. Phone: (415) 771-2022. Hours: 6 a.m. to 2 a.m. M/F: 99/1.

This place is the same as it was almost ten years ago when Pansy first started cruising Polk Street. The bathrooms are scummy but cruisy with action hampered by lack of a door. The patrons include buckets of hookers, rough trade, TVs and TSs—welcome to Polk Street. The very small interior is painted red and is quite dark and gloomy. Televisions feature everything from porno film clips (up to the good part) to 911 shows. Many of the patrons seem to still be deluded into believing that ripping one's own blue jeans with a Cuisinart is very sexy. On our last visit, the very cute bartender kept giving Betty the eye. When we left to do more reviewing, he almost had a heart attack. Betty ducked back in to give him her phone number. He never called. Betty, however, has spotted him several times working Collingwood Park (see Cruising, page 87) with a fury rivaled by few. We recently spotted him at a straight bar three sheets to the wind. When queens go down the stony end—no one is safe. Despite it all, Polk Gulch remains one of the busiest and most popular bars on Polk. Best time to visit is weekend nights.

P.S. Piano Bar

1121 Polk bet. Post and Sutter. Phone: (415) 885-1448.
Hours: 6 a.m. to 2 a.m. M/F: 99/1.

The P.S. now has piano music Wednesday and Thursday, 9 p.m. to 1 a.m.; Friday and Saturday, 9 p.m. to 1 a.m.; and Sunday, 5 to 9 p.m. We were informed by our pal Dan Seitler that the piano in question is more of an organ. Perhaps P.S. Wurlitzer Bar would be more apropos. The barkeep was quiet and friendly. The interior is home to an infinite mirror tunnel, a ton of blue neon (blinding, in fact), faux chateau-style windows, and a circular bar that takes up about half the space. Patrons are mostly older guys staring into their drinks with the occasional hustler just passing through. Despite our many visits, we have never seen this place come close to being busy. All in all, P.S. is a true adventure.

Q.T. II

1312 Polk at Bush. Phone: (415) 885-1114. Hours: noon to 2 a.m. M/F: 85/15.

This used to be our all-time favorite bar on Polk Street. The staff was great, the music was great, the crowd was seedy but entertaining and the drinks were Polk Street Punches. This perfect formula has disappeared. The staff of today has never heard of a Polk Street Punch and certainly do not know how to make one. The oddly comfortable carpeted bleachers were long ago replaced by tall cocktail tables and chairs. Other interior details include: a large video screen, rainbow flags, stage trimmed with fancy disco lighting, and magic with bathroom mirror tiles. Patrons consist of hustlers and daddies looking for same. The bathroom wins no points for cleanliness or privacy. Obtain a key from the bartender for the women's room if you require privacy. The most exciting aspect of the Q.T. of late is the amateur strip contest on Tuesday evenings at 9 p.m. Occasionally no one signs up, and the most drunk and/or poorest patron volunteers as he is assured the seventy-five-dollar winnings. The professional strippers perform Sundays at 9 p.m. but they are not as fun. A sign posted in the window did mention that these models were available for *private parties* (emphasis ours). The live musical performances on Friday evenings from 9:30 p.m. to 1:30 a.m. are often quite enjoyable and include pop rock, rhythm and blues, jazz, Top Forty and flashback.

Reflections

1160 Polk at Sutter. Phone: (415) 771-6262.
Hours: 6 a.m. to 2 a.m. M/F: 100/0.

A.k.a. Rejections. When there is a doorman, he is generally strict about carding. The bathroom reminded Betty of the closet in *Carrie*—the one Momma forced Carrie to pray to Jesus in regarding her "dirty pillows." Betty spotted a weeble, who almost wobbled right over Betty exiting the bathroom, nearly killing her. It's the most vile, disgusting bathroom ever. There are pinball machines, computer games and a very active pool table. There seems to be a straight/gay dichotomy—straights play pool and gays drink. Bartenders are friendly. The L-shaped bar is spacious with a beveled mirror behind it. The television screens occasionally feature teaser videos—porn films right up to the point where actual sex occurs and then a music video or another film. The crowd mostly consisted of working-class stiffs and a lot of hustlers and other Polk Street rough-trade types. Besides the influx of straight people, there also seems to be a wave of C&W music. Reflections was under construction on our most recent visit. They appear to be renovating for wheelchair accessibility to the pool table as it is at a slightly higher level than the rest of the bar. This is certainly commendable but they have failed to notice that there are several steps to enter the bar and no disabled person could ever use their tiny bathroom. These folks are so in touch with the needs of the physically impaired these days, their televisions are all close-captioned. Too bad they weren't able to hear Kenny Rogers belting out "These Are a Few of My Favorite Things." We had to.

Rendezvous

1303 Polk at Bush. Phone: (415) 673-7934.
Hours: 9 a.m. to 2 a.m. M/F: 90/10.

The interior at the Rendezvous includes televisions, oodles of gay pride hoo ha, and tall cocktail tables and stools. They self-advertise that they are the "Home of the Greatest Forty-Niner Parties and Fans in SF." They are not kidding. Their devotion to the team ranges from posters and pennants on the wall to Forty-Niner brunches to drink specials during games. The donations from brunch go to the AIDS Emergency Fund. It seems like a quiet, friendly place for sports queens. Jeans and sporty tops seem to be the uniform of choice. The bartender was cute and friendly. One bathroom was not so clean and allowed no privacy. If you require privacy, ask the bartender for the key to the other restroom. Best time to visit is during Forty-Niner games.

The Swallow

1750 Polk bet. Clay and Washington.
Phone: (415) 775-4152. Hours: 10 a.m. to 2 a.m. M/F: 95/5.

This lively piano bar is peopled with a crowd of older gents. The seats and tables are tall cocktail variety. All in all, this is a beautiful atmosphere with a lot of pep. Piano players are on the keys six nights a week. Tuesday is the only silent night. The patrons consist of elderly regulars, show-tune queens, and some women (including a cocktail waitress). The bartenders are friendly and wonderful. Betty adores the bathroom. The door on the stall is a real door that you can close and lock for complete privacy. Francine Lumbert and Pansy had a lovely time at The Swallow drinking port after Pansy's forty-first birthday dinner. The bartender asked them incredulously if they had just happened in off the street. He was pleasantly surprised that they chose it as a quiet, lovely place to chat and listen to show tunes on the piano while business-district types cast aside their inhibitions (after a few belts of gin) to suddenly start channeling Barbra Streisand. Easily the classiest act on all of Polk Street.

The Wooden Horse

622 Polk at Turk. Phone: (415) 441-9278. Hours: 6 a.m. to 2 a.m. M/F: 90/10.

The first time we visited this minute bar, we witnessed four guys playing Yahtzee as the jukebox played Nana Maskouri's "I'm Your Lady." The crescent-shaped bar might seat a half dozen regular-sized folks. It is known as "The funniest little small bar north of Market Street." On our recent visit, Pansy was anxious to ensure that the confessional screen was still in the bathroom. Eureka! Betty was more than slightly disturbed that they still have a Teddy Skill Crane. During our initial research, simply ages ago, approximately ninety-nine percent of all gay bars in SF had one. Now they must be the rarest of antiques—smart investment on the part of The Wooden Horse. The Wooden Horse has been featuring the smallest drag shows in San Francisco. The stage is the size of a dinner tray and the bar itself is the size of an average living room.

S O M A

See Maps, page 174.

Eagle

398 12th St. at Harrison. Phone: (415) 626-0880.
Hours: Mon thru Fri, opens at 4 p.m.; Sat at 2 p.m.; Sun at noon; always closes at
2 a.m. M/F: 99/1.

The symbol of the eagle evokes images ranging from majes-
tic birds of prey to featherless, pink baby birds gagging with
hunger. Oops, that inadvertently describes a variety of
patrons at a typical Sunday afternoon beer bust at the Eagle,
"San Francisco's Premier Leather Bar." Like smudged,
streaked, Tom of Finland sketches, the ideal is blurred and
contorted into an affable crowd of ruddy-cheeked, concrete
actualities. The leather fetish is carried a bit too far at times
though, until the beer bust blend of sunlight and booze cures
the skin to a porous, blotchy, red leather substitute. Among
the crowd you can find more tops and bottoms than on a sale
rack at Esprit. From kinky raunchy pigs to vinyl, vanilla
wannabes, there truly is something for everyone. Prepare
yourself for a time-warp of sorts, where passion still res-
onates with funky disco rhythms, and hankies still ooze with
meaning, among other things. The Eagle has three bars, an
outdoor patio, stage, heat lamps, pinball and billiards—like
Chuck E Cheese only with smegma. The SF Eagle is not for
the weak of heart, pregnant women or adult children of alcoholics. The best time to visit is always the Sunday afternoon
beer bust from 3 to 6 p.m. There is a cover.

The EndUp

401 6th St. at Harrison. Phone: (415) 543-7700. Hours: see below. Cover: varies.

This gay historic spot was well-known for its wet jockey
short contests of the seventies. This pinnacle of gay history
was highlighted in the PBS series *Tales of the City.* It is also
former home to the greatest club ever to hit San Francisco—
Uranus (R.I.P.). Lately this space has become a Rent-a-Club,
a different club every night of the week. Thursday nights
seem to appeal to a (gasp) straight crowd. For several years
Friday nights were for gay boys and Saturday nights for lesbians, but not lately. Last year, rumors raced like wildfire that
The EndUp was closing forever and folks packed the place in
droves for one last sketchy weekend. The surge of business

saved it in the nick of time but it still seems like it is floundering. About the only time this is just The EndUp anymore is the tea dance on Saturday, Sunday and Monday mornings starting at 6 a.m. People actually drag their butts there at 6 a.m. when they can't quite come down by dawn. Since this is the only place open, folks often end up here (get it?). The space is great: a dance floor, fireplace, pool table, pinball machine, back deck and waterfall. For more details see Clubs, Spaces, page 83.

French Quarter

201 9th St. at Howard. Phone: DNA. Hours: DNA. M/F: 80/20.

What the hell is going on here? This bar was once known as the Underground and then The Pit/Cocktails and then Phillip's French Quarter. When we visited, their liquor license was gone but they were open. Also, the phone number for Phillip's French Quarter has been disconnected. Also, rumors are running rampant that it is going out of business or has changed hands yet again. We wish someone would scoop this gem up and stabilize it. The upstairs houses a small restaurant with after-hours food, a long and gorgeous wooden bar, rows of pinball machines, bathrooms, a pool table and plenty of seating. The downstairs is host to a large dance floor with a low ceiling, another bar, more bathrooms, and a DJ booth. Remember when you were in the closet and you envisioned what a seedy underground gay bar must be like? This is the place, except you got over your internalized homophobia and now you're loving it. The French Quarter does not really have a regular crowd. It is often home to clubs on different nights of the week. The upside is that the dance floor is open twenty-four hours a day on the weekends. Sometimes the party is raging and other times is haunted by eerie fan dancers of yesteryear.

Ginger's Too

43 6th St. at Market. Phone: (415) 543-3622.
Hours: 10 a.m. to 2 a.m. M/F: 100/0.

"Downtown Inexpensive Drinking Bar for People with Money" is their motto. Herb Caen called it "Casual Dining in Wino Country." A sign over the bar indicates cigar and pipe smoking are not allowed. Pictures of drag queens from yesteryear also decorate the wall behind the bar. The jukebox played mostly C&W songs. Without warning, the jukebox broke with tradition spewing forth the following medley: Village People's "Macho Man," Jeanette McDonald's (known for opening her golden gates) "San Francisco," Village People's "YMCA," Sinatra's "Strangers in the Night," and Englebert Humperdinck's "After the Loving." The interior consists of: Shakey's Pizza-style tiffany lamps with dust motes the size of your head, brown stucco ceiling, non-functional dance floor decorated with bathroom mirror tiles, cut-out rainbows and fluffy clouds hanging over the bar, and piano. The bathroom was like totally grody—oh ma godddd. On weekend mornings, Aunt Sophie's Kitchen (?) serves food (i.e. hash and eggs, $5.95). The Horny Devil Sting was $1.50—same price as the red ribbon buttons.

Hole in the Wall

289 8th St. bet. Howard and Folsom. Phone: (415) 431-HOWL. Hours: 6 a.m. to 2 a.m. M/F: 80/20.

The Hole in the Wall is self-billed as a "Nasty Little Biker Bar." The bar that you *never* wanted to go to is now the bar you *need* to go to. On our recent visit, it seemed like old home week. We ran into people we have not seen since Uranus died. The rock and roll music is slamming and there is always a DJ on duty. The music is diverse (from Jane's Addiction to Led Zeppelin) while the video montages range from Ab Fab to Japanese animation on television screens covered with colored gels. Try ordering a beer or Jack Daniels shots—no drinks with umbrellas, lady. Although cruising occurs, it is more of a hangout than a cruise bar. Folks are talking, not posing. On a recent visit, a no-name drag queen spotted Betty across the room and began dishing her. She was mighty embarrassed to discover she was dishing Betty to none other than Pansy. Our spy Naomi tells us that there is a regular nicknamed Unga Bungan. He tends to pull his dick out at the bar and masturbate for awhile. Then he takes a snack break and dips his hand in the Chex Mix on the bar. Then he returns to masturbating. In any event, DON'T EAT THE CHEX MIX. Although several motorcycle clubs hold special events here, you don't need to own a motorcycle to enjoy it. If there is a line however, show up with a motorcycle helmet for priority. Also, if you have a helmet, show your dick or your ass, you are bound to get happy-hour prices or perhaps a free drink. Exhibitionism is not only tolerated here, it is encouraged. Barbie and Pansy once spotted Lucy (Australio Pithicus) foraging at the bar. The ghost of Jerome is still running from one end of the bar to the other.

Lonestar Saloon

1354 Harrison bet. 9th and 10th Sts. Phone: (415) 863-9999.
Hours: Mon thru Fri 12 p.m. to 2 a.m., Sat and Sun. 9 a.m. to 2 a.m. M/F: 98/2.

We love it! The staff and clientele are friendly despite appearances to the contrary. Picture Big Bird, Barney and the Hey
Kool-Aid pitcher smoking stogies in a circle jerk, team-tit-
tweak formation, and you have got a pretty accurate image
of the Lonestar's back patio scene on any given day. Music
at the Lonestar is arguably the best in town—raucous rock
and roll to wiggle and jiggle by. The lighting is absolutely
fabulous, which is somewhat incongruous for a butch bar.
The barrel of peanuts is a nice touch but don't indulge if you
are having a herpetic outbreak. There are pinball and computer games and a busy pool table. The trough-style urinals
are extremely cruisy. Ask for Matt, the super great barkeep.
On our recent visit, Pansy was brained by the descending
projection screen near the pool table. We got all excited for
some hot porn but were treated instead to footage of air
shows (you know, airplanes taking off, flying around and
landing). We were thrilled by the spectacle. Thank god,
someone caught it on video, distributed it, sold it. Thank god,
the Lonestar bought it, and played it when we were there. It
changed our lives. We laughed, we cried, it was much better
than *Cats.* If you are on the net, visit the Lonestar's home
page: http://www.lonestar.saloon.com.

My Place

1225 Folsom bet. 8th and 9th Sts. Phone: (415) 863-2329.
Hours: Mon thru Fri 10 a.m. to 2 a.m., Sat and Sun 6 a.m. to 2 a.m. M/F: 100/0.

"Your Place to Cruise and Drink Cheap!!" is their slogan.
Thursday night is leather night: you gotta be in leather. Drink
specials every day. This is a heavy cruise bar. Leather crowd
likes to drink and hang out here. Though they advertise certain days and times as a sleazefest, any time at My Place is
a sleazefest. In case you are clueless as to what the bar is
about, the hot humpy porn vids should give you a clue. Since
the "alley" has been closed, folks have decided to have sex
right in the middle of the bar. The bartenders don't seem to
mind until the action spills over into their personal work
space. The bathroom is so damn cruisy that pissing is sec-
ondary to blowjobs. Occasionally, the barback will bellow, "If
you're not pissing get out of the bathroom." A pool table has
been added but it just seems like one more thing to fuck

around or over. On the wall, there is a great painting, called *Man's Country,* which is, according to Pansy, from a late-sixties SF bar. We, however, prefer to call it *Gay Blind Clones.* The music is great and is deejayed from behind the bar by the bartender himself. It is generally good no matter who is working.

Best time to visit is midnight (it's cruisy and friendly). Remember the first time our friend Naomi visited here? She heard it was a leather bar so she wore pleated, black slacks; a white, rayon, long-sleeved T-shirt; and black patent leather shoes. When she awoke the next morning from a blackout in front of My Place, it was Folsom Street Fair Day. They were towing her car and she raced to bribe the tow-truck driver. She realized as she was handing him forty dollars that she was holding her underwear in her other hand. Remember the time Miss Jerome was running around in scary polyester businessman drag? Remember the time the S.F.P.D. burst in the bar, headed straight to the alley and started carding and handcuffing queens? Remember the time we visited on Christmas night and Pansy had the honor of becoming the creamy filling of an oreo cookie? Remember the time Pansy was blowing that stud who pissed in Ms. Pansy's mouth without consent? She did not know what to do with her piss-filled cheeks so she kissed the jerk full on the mouth and he drank his own steamy load? He drank it right down like Gandhi. Glug, glug. Joan Jett Blakk opines to Pansy, "And he's still in love with you, girl."

Powerhouse

1347 Folsom bet. 9th and 10th Sts. Phone: (415) 552-8689.
Hours: Mon thru Fri 4 p.m. to 2 a.m., Sat and Sun 10 a.m. to 2 a.m. M/F: 99/1.

A.k.a. The Powder Room. Long, long ago when Pansy and Betty did not know each other, there was another, earlier, butcher Powerhouse. Pansy used to bring her dates there. Betty only visited once, in an effort to garner political support for a same-sex marriage proposition on the ballot. She was called a "twinkie" by one gentleman and another refused to sign anything because "they use those lists when they get ready to ship us off to the camps." The interior is pretty much the same as the original. There is a pool table and a backyard that has potential and seems unfinished at the time of our review. Most of the patrons were serious as a heart attack about the world of dead cow flesh. We have been waiting for years for gorgeous gay men to fetishize cotton. There were some hot dudes there but everyone was so busy posing as hyperbutch that not a lot of "love connections" were being made. Two losers beside us (the Bob & Rod of San José) had spray painted some acid-wash jeans on their beefy thighs and bubble butts and made their way into the city. While we were taking a smoking break on the back deck, a lovely gaunt gentleman strolled out with a leather-hooded slave on a leash. He seemed so menacing until he had to ask Pansy for a light. There are rumors of a dungeon but we witnessed no such thing. Dream on, tampon. The bartenders were very friendly and cute. We fought the whole time about who would receive the honor of tongue bathing their tight twitching holes. We thought the tearoom action would be hot in such a spot. Betty, however, totally intimidated all the leather queens with her sophisticated, aggressive tearoom mating rituals. Betty was all over it like a chicken on a wounded worm; they didn't know what hit them. Tuesday nights are *noche de cuero* (Latins in leather). There are beer busts on Wednesday nights from 6 to 10 p.m. and Sundays from noon to 10 p.m.

Rawhide II

280 7th St. at Harrison. Phone: (415) 621-1197.
Hours: 11 a.m. to 2 a.m. M/F: 70/30.

The Rawhide is a very popular C&W bar. Gay men and women in their thirties to forties are always dancing in full-on C&W drag. The huge U.S. flag hanging over the dance floor was less than pleasant. No locks on the bathroom doors (both "studs" and "fillies") is not acceptable. Recently we visited and noticed the mounted heads of many dead creatures of the forest and plain near the pool table. Deeply disturbing. One was Bambi's mother. We downed our drinks served by a very friendly bartender. The coat-check slave was quite a chipper lad with some time on his hands. Pansy noted that he was reading *The Te of Piglet*—always an important resource when you work at the Rawhide. We decided to bail A.S.A.P. but Betty had the call of nature upon her. She waited impatiently for the Studs bathroom and finally decided upon the Fillies. As we were gathering our coats, the bathroom hog emerged. It was some bovine cowboy wannabe in a Stetson and extremely loud shirt. He headed toward the dance floor but turned and walked behind the bar to bark at a few of the employees. Oh no. We left.

The Stud

399 9th St. at Harrison. Phone: (415) 863-6623.
Hours: 5 p.m. to 2 a.m. (after-hours on Fri and Sat). Cover: varies. M/F: 85/15.

This place is an institution in San Francisco. Unfortunately it is always in flux. Things were stable for awhile until one of the owners fell out his window and died. Scary, huh? After that, things were on the upswing for awhile when they housed Klubstitute (R.I.P.), Junk (R.I.P.), and a few other temporarily homeless clubs. Now the best night of the week seems to be Sunday's retro night. Interior is a lot of fun: assorted license plates, totem poles, year round X-mas lights, antique mirrors, working electric train circles above the bar ablaze with Yarzeit candles. Black light dance floor. Friendly coat check. Dismal bathrooms with some cruise potential in the one by the coat check. Very loud, danceable music. Collegiate crowd reminds Betty of her Boston days. Wednesday night is oldies night with $1.00 cover and $1.25 domestic beers, and is the best night to visit for boys. The pool table and row of pinball machines are always occupied.

VSF

278 11th St. at Folsom. Phone: (415) 621-1531.
Hours: 4 p.m. to 2 a.m. (after-hours on weekends). Cover: $10.00. M/F: 65/35.

Long, long ago, this was a bathhouse. Urban gay myth tells the tale that some queen died here while trying to do poppers underneath the water in the pool. In the eighties, it was transformed into a bar and the pool was covered over to form a dance floor. Folks were always concerned that if the dance floor got too full they would crash through and drown. This bar has changed hands many times and we always hoped someone would snatch up this fabulous space and make it a seven-day-a-week gay bar. Well, some of our prayers were answered and some were not. Some group of wealthy faggy investors bought it and refurbished it. They filled in the pool which is now a lovely sunken dance floor. They have redone the lights, the sound, and completely redecorated with a vengeance. The dance floor is great. In all the years that Pansy has been away from home (Miami), she has never come close to seeing anything that touched the Miami experience. ¡This bar está muy Cubanisima! Plants, drapes, Roosevelt-era murals, columns, plush carpeting, semi-circular booths and a staff that would probably be more at home on the runway or in *Details* magazine (the Miami edition).

All this restoration and redecoration are great, however, we have a couple bones to pick. First of all, ten dollars, please. Second of all, class issues much? They have valet parking. How many gay bars in San Francisco have valet parking? They finally filled the desperate void. We gave them our roller skates and said take good care of them. Thirdly, YOU ARE NOT ALLOWED TO SMOKE INSIDE but you are allowed to gag continuously on the non-stop fog emanating from the fog machine off the dance floor. So half the bar was huddled in the rain on the roof trying to have a cig. Though they do not yet seem to be dragging in a large or regular crowd, they are wising up. They are starting to host clubs, which will certainly make folks more familiar with the new digs. This is supposed to be the new home of GirlSpot. While we were there, the crowd was thin, co-gender, largely middle-class, young, and apparently from out of town.

TENDERLOIN

See Maps, page 170.

Aunt Charlie's Lounge

133 Turk at Taylor. Phone: (415) 441-2922. Hours: 6 a.m. to 2 a.m. M/F: 99/1.

This is a mini-Tenderloin version of Midnight Sun with disturbing similarities. There are two computer games, one pinball machine, a CD jukebox and two televisions (one large screen), but no pool table. The mirror tunnel is an experience. This is a warm and friendly space. There is no impending threat of death, which is odd for the Tenderloin. The interior consists of pink neon and tall cocktail tables and stools. The well-lit restroom includes a broken throne and a big mirror for coif fixin'.

The Hob Nob

700 Geary at Leavenworth. Phone: (415) 771-9866.
Hours: 6 a.m. to 2 a.m. M/F: 100/0.

We met this lovely guy named Bill who panhandled our friend Kevbob before we even sat down. When Kevbob adjourned to the powder room, Bill spotted Betty's bright, shining, smiling face and meandered right over and plopped himself down. He told us his whole hard-luck life story about how he had been up for three days and people kept buying beers for him but wouldn't give him money for food. So, Betty said, "Honey, I'll give you money for food but only when you leave." In the interim, Betty gave him a cigarette. Bill ripped the filter right off and smoked that cig down to a nub.

Betty noticed that there had been some redecoration since her last visit. There are now oil paintings on display with post-it notes announcing respective prices. The walls have been repainted, and the establishment has employed that omnipresent technique of decorating with bathroom tile mirrors. The barkeep was as friendly as all heck. The same six guys that were here two years ago were in attendance. One of the patrons upon leaving passed our table. Before Bill could even lift his head from his drunken haze, the man barked, "Hey, that's your problem, not mine, buddy!" He knew what Bill's issue was. He also barked, "You're in the wrong company!" As if Bill became a Boy Scout now, he would not be homeless. Doy!

Kokpit

301 Turk at Leavenworth. Phone: (415) 774-3260.
Hours: 6 a.m. to 2 a.m. M/F: 80/20.

One night we arrived at about eleven p.m. and the bartender informed us that the bar was closing. We assumed they hated us, our clothing or our people, but when we returned later to check up on that suspicious claim, they were in fact closed. There are occasional drag shows here. The stage is the size of a postage stamp. Lots of out-of-towners come here as the bartender told us it is known as the "World Famous Kokpit." The best time to visit is any afternoon during the week. There is no pool table but there are pinball machines and computer games. Pansy once visited with her friends Marky Mark Duran Duran and Barbie during the afternoon. The bar was packed and everyone was very friendly. They were all invited to play some game at the bar that involved money. The bartender was helpful and courteous and they were not treated like strangers.

McDonald's Pub

1108B Market at 7th St. Phone: (415) 861-1847.
Hours: 6 a.m. (but sometimes as late at 10 a.m.) to 2 a.m. M/F: 60/40.

We heard a vicious rumor that we had actually *missed* a gay bar in San Francisco. We immediately rocketed over to the address to investigate. McDonald's is located in a neighborhood that can best be described as seedy. Our initial observation was that McDonald's was only two doors down from the McDonald's with the golden arches. In fact, the Renoir hotel is sandwiched between two McDonald's. Coincidence or God's grand design? When we ordered our drinks from the cheerful bartendress we still weren't sure it was a gay bar. Though there were some obvious queens and a big dyke couple, there were also random straight folks including one oppressively sloppy couple trading spit while waiting for a cab. While searching desperately for confirmation, we found an interesting poster on the bulletin board. It explained to the women reading it that the I.R.S. was not after them but their employer "Bijou." This tipped us off to the fact that a chunk of the clientele is employed at the nearby "theaters." The music was rocking out of the CD jukebox with rainbow lights (a clue?). As we were watching *Serial Mom*, a large photo montage caught our attention. The center screamed "Gay Rights Now." The pictures all seemed to hearken back to seventies' Gay Pride marches likening Anita Bryant to Adolf Hitler and Stalin (only they could sing better). All in all, if you want to slum it, are a lap dancer, or need a shot after you down your Big Mac—this is the place. Happy hour every day 8 to 10 a.m. and Mon thru Fri 4 to 7 p.m. TV spots, pinball machines, pool table, video games, 16 oz. draft beer for $2.00.

UPPER MARKET

See Maps, page 160.

Galleon

718 14th St. at Market and Church. Phone: (415) 431-0253.
Hours: 3 p.m. to 2 a.m. M/F: 90/10.

This is a piano bar with a full-service restaurant that likes to bill itself as "The Premier San Francisco Supper Club." There is a live piano player most evenings of the week. Cabaret on Friday nights, Jazz on Saturday nights, Leather two-for-one on Wednesday nights. Sometimes the patrons eat; sometimes the patrons sing. Pricey drinks. Half the crowd were extras in the San Francisco run of *Joseph and the Amazing Technicolor Dream Coat.* Bathroom is clean, well-lit and personal. Safe space for drag queens and straight people. On our way out of The Transfer one night, we actually witnessed two fat queens tanked to the gills being bodily dragged out of the Galleon, handcuffed and unceremoniously stuffed in the back seat of an S.F.P.D. cruiser. Did they sing off key or demand a rendition of "Seasons in the Sun"?

The Mint

1942 Market near Guerrero. Phone: (415) 626-4726.
Hours: 11 a.m. to 2 a.m. M/F: 85/15.

This place has become one of the hottest spots in town. Why? Because it is the only queer karaoke bar in San Francisco. It is too funny and ironic to watch some queen get up and sing "Wind Beneath My Wings" to a queer audience while a soft-core heterosexual Japanese version of the song is projected onto the screen behind her. The bathroom is clean and affords privacy. People will be especially nice to you if you tell the VJ (video jockey) that it is your first time. Everyone has to have a first time and The Mint is as gentle a teacher as you are apt to find. Even if you don't sing, and please don't let anyone make you think that you have to, you can still have a good time watching the show. There is a two-drink minimum during karaoke hours (every day 9 p.m. to 2 a.m. and Sundays 4 p.m. to 2 a.m.). The mixed drinks are served weak, so choose beer or wine. A burger joint next door connects to the bar. You can eat at the restaurant (which serves excellent shakes and fries) or bring your food into the bar. For dinner and a show, it's hard to beat the Mint.

Pilsner

225 Church at Market. Phone: (415) 621-7058.
Hours: Mon thru Fri 9 a.m. to 2 a.m., Sat and Sun 7 a.m. to 2 a.m. M/F: 90/10.

This seems to be a semi-popular neighborhood bar. More a place for a beer and chat with a friend than a cruise spot. The nicest interior detail is the ceiling. Walls are bench-lined. Pansy noted the antique wooden phone booth. The totally spotless tearoom has some potential as there is a trough urinal equipped with mirror, but it is wasted due to a propped open door with glass window (boo hoo). The pool table is especially nice and on Mondays 6 to 10 p.m. pool is free of charge. There are lots of pinball machines and computer games. This is the only bar that we have ever seen that has a Lotto machine—what is up with that? We have heard a disturbing rumor from some friends. Allegedly, this bar will give you a free beer in exchange for your AA chip. Pardon us? Pray it is not true because in most cultures (including this one) that would be considered *tacky.*

The Transfer

198 Church at Market and 14th St. Phone: (415) 861-7499. Hours: Mon thru Fri 11 a.m. to 2 a.m., Sat and Sun 6 a.m. to 2 a.m. M/F: 90/10.

This is a small bar with a friendly, peppy ambiance, nice staff, and music with a beat. The bathroom is generally not so tidy, with no tearoom potential or privacy. The place is peppered with barrels for tables; the three televisions never seem to be on. There is an electronic information guide and a nice neon clock over the bar. There are several pinball machines, computer games and one pool table that is taken quite seriously (note the giant rock o' chalk). Pool tournaments are from 3 to 5 p.m. every Sunday. Best time to visit is weekends.

OTHER NEIGHBORHOODS

Alta Plaza

2301 Fillmore near California. Neighborhood: Pacific Heights. Map: pg.165.
Phone: (415) 922-1444. Hours: Mon thru Sat 4 p.m. to 2 a.m., Sun 10 a.m. to 2 a.m.
M/F: 98/2.

A.k.a. Altar of Plastic, The Ultra Spastic, etc. It was the place to meet A-Gays (when they were still around) and find husbands "of means and substance." Unfortunately, the Plaza of today is just a shell of its former self. Those seeking tuition checks still gravitate toward the well-dressed and well-heeled but are having trouble finding the well-bred. The crowd consists of many white guys in starched white shirts, self-consciously standing around acting like they have important places to go. It is the only bar in town where there is absolutely no movement. The drill goes like this: find your spotlight, stand and pose for the remainder of the evening, mug for the crowd and have one of the cocktail waiters bring you drinks. None of the men have facial hair and there are very few women here. Usually, it's someone's sister (literally) or some executive-assistant Fag Hag.

The drinks are watered down, the glassware is passable, and the music is all but inconsequential. Still, it remains one of the most lovely bars to see. There are tasteful furnishings, brass, mirrors, wood, a medium L-shaped bar and the best lighting in the city. Everybody looks about seven to ten years younger in here. With two levels of standing and seating areas, the setting is ideal for finding your prey, measuring him up and then going in for the kill. The bar has an entrance on Fillmore Street and is connected to a restaurant of very minor reputation. If you have friends visiting from out of town, this may be just the place to bring them to drink, air kiss, and call each other darling. As Andrew Sullivan might say, everyone here is virtually normal.

The staff is extremely attentive. So attentive, in fact, that on Betty's most recent visit they started quoting our review of them. They did fill her with free booze so she has to say these dudes are okay. She and her friend Steve met a gentleman who was having a moral quandary. He had just been offered a job as a fur salesman and didn't know if folks would think less of him. Speaking of the Altar of Plastic, they are the only gay bar we are aware of that takes Mastercard, VISA, AMEX and Discover (Discover?).

Chances

298 Divisadero at Page. Neighborhood: The Haight. Map: pg. 164.
Phone: (415) 255-6101. Hours: 5 p.m. to 2 a.m.

Ssshhh. This is the best kept secret in the city. It also happens to be B&P's neighborhood bar. We and all our friends and roommates frequent it. So now it is an even more fabulous place to hang. Lots of good beer on tap and drunks and pool-playing dykes and bowling on television. If there are girls in the house, the jukebox plays *good* music. Yeah. Most important, of course, is the pinball machine, which lurks by the lower pool table in the back, luring unsuspecting accomplices into its nefarious scheme to corrupt the youth of our fair city. Or maybe that's just Betty. It seems that all these Haight-ish scruffy "straight" boys suddenly have the pinball bug, and flock to the once-abandoned and lonely machine now that our esteemed authoress is on the scene. Betty offers this rule of thumb, since all of them look the same: the faggots *have* the comb, which the straight boys request, in their back pocket; the straight boys say "sweet" when they get the needed beauty device. If you take the time and make this bar your own, you too can name the closet cases. Our favorites are Greg Brady, Lucan Garrett (Leif's wolfish younger bro) and Honey Mustard (as in, "I'd like to dip those legs in honey mustard sauce").

The straight-girl bartenders are the coolest. Since the bar recently opened, they're still very strict about I.D., but, if you're in a bind, just say "April, you already carded me!!!" If April's not working, you're shit out of luck. Quincy will play pinball with you and will sport the quarters for quite a few games if you're lucky. If you hear that "California Dreaming" song on the jukebox, be careful, and follow duck-and-cover procedures, or just evacuate. This means that Tracy, who just moved to California, is, as they say, "in the house."

Company

1319 California at Leavenworth. Neighborhood: Nob Hill. Map: pg. 170.
Phone: (415) 928-0677. Hours: Mon thru Fri 4 p.m. to 2 a.m., Sat and Sun 2 p.m.
to 2 a.m.

Company is one the most tasteful and quiet gay bars in the city. They have an extremely clean bathroom—powder fresh. Only use the stall, however, if you are a contortionist or a midget. The door is approximately one foot from the toilet. To sit comfortably, one must keep the stall door open with your knees, or simply wrap your ankles around your neck. This place is always filled with stealth freaks, which means they seem normal at first. Everybody, and we mean everybody, knows each other. No matter where customers are sitting in the bar, and it is not a tiny bar, they speak to each other as if they are all deaf and sitting at the same table. They still have an extensive drink menu BUT they a) don't know how to make them and b) don't have the materials and c) are not good at substituting. Also, they put ice in Pansy's drink after she specifically requested, in no uncertain terms, that she wanted *no ice in her drink*. They are nice though, even if a bit 'tarded. Company is one of the oddest places we have visited. We have never met or spoken to anyone who has visited or even heard of this establishment. Never, never. What keeps it open? We do not know.

The Gate

1093 Pine at Jones. Neighborhood: Nob Hill. Map: pg. 170. Phone: (415) 885-2852. Hours: 4 p.m. to 2 a.m., weekends and holidays 11 a.m. to 2 a.m. M/F: 70/30.

The Gate is a small, cute neighborhood bar with an adjoining restaurant. The space is open and airy. The interior consists of a brick wall, a non-functional yet decorative balcony, a horseshoe-shaped bar with a foot rest, tastefully hung framed mirrors, and small tables by the windows. The Gate is a great space that seems horribly underutilized and is mostly frequented by neighbors, a pretty mixed straight/gay clientele. The bathroom is clean and tidy. The CD jukebox has a great selection of tunes. Our Nob Hill Spy Tom informs us that The Gate is host to Chili/Bingo on Mondays at 7 p.m. Though the sign that used to announce the event is now gone, Tom reports that when he passes by on Mondays, queens are lined up with bingo cards and cups o' chili, so it sounds like the special evening is still in full force.

Ginger's Trois

246 Kearny at Bush. Neighborhood: Financial District. Map: pg. 171.
Phone: (415) 989-0282. Hours: Mon thru Fri 10 a.m. to 10 p.m. M/F: 100/0.

Since the closing of Sutter's Mill, this now reigns as the only gay bar downtown. Parking is a total nightmare especially during rush-hour traffic. Ginger's Trois is a great place to go for a drink if you work downtown and if you are already with fun people, because you won't meet fun people in this dive. Mason, the "happy-hour" bartender, is a riot and makes the best margaritas downtown. Mason is a southern-belle artist whose work is at Off Your Dot (in the Castro). He also has a soft spot for sappy country music which he plays for your enjoyment when the piano player is absent. Sometimes there is live piano music, and all the old queens sing along. If anyone gets out of control, Mason has a croquet mallet that he loves to bang on the bar to demand order. The scene is always pretty surreal, especially in a bar with smoked mirror walls covered with silhouettes of Fred and Ginger dancing. The bottom line is that Ginger's Trois can be a lot of fun, but is certainly not a pick-up bar unless you are a senior citizen, alcoholic, or downtown hotel resident.

The Lion Pub

2062 Divisadero at Sacramento. Neighborhood: Pacific Heights. Map: pg. 165. Phone: (415) 567-6565. Hours: noon to 2 a.m. M/F: 98/2.

A.k.a. The Lion's Den, The Lion Queen, The Lying Queen. The Lion has been drained of expensive-cocktail-purchasing queens ever since the Alta Plaza reopened. One would assume that this city has enough Clinique-counter boys to keep two four-dollar-a-domestic-beer bars open and thriving. The high points of this pub include the lovely fireplace, reminiscent of hunting lodges, and the active pick-up quotient. If you prefer a Stanford vice president as an escort, then this place should suit your needs. We especially appreciate the pretty bartenders in tight black T-shirts, much like those worn at faggy, upscale hair salons. This is the kind of bar that queers bring their relatives and straight friends to when they want to prove that gay bars are not dens of iniquity.

Marlena's

488 Hayes at Octavia. Neighborhood: Hayes Valley. Map: pg. 165. Phone: (415) 864-6672. Hours: Mon thru Fri noon to 2 a.m., Sat and Sun 10 a.m. to 2 a.m. M/F: 95/5.

We just left Marlena's, which was rocking tonight. It was all about the *Priscilla Queen of the Desert* soundtrack, and the muted colors were so subtle that we almost didn't notice them. We think the bartender was Marlena herself—someone kept calling him Marlena but he didn't look like no Marlena. The bathrooms have no cruise potential unless you bring someone in with you. The urinal's very sloppy and there was piss on the floor. Marlena (or was it really?) stood behind Pansy while she tinkled…scared of that. There is still a Keno machine and a CD juke box, but the clientele has been jacked up about eight and a half registers from last time. There were a handful of neighborhood types and more than a handful of guppies. We spotted at least one drag-queen (Emma), who kept our cover, and lots of drag queen wannabes. Fernando liked it and he was only drinking water. They have a mirror tunnel just like Double Rainbow. Lots of cute boys and lots of scary guys. There is one pool table that people put to use.

Trax

1437 Haight bet. Ashbury and Masonic. Neighborhood: The Haight. Map: pg. 164. Phone: (415) 864-4213. Hours: noon to 2 a.m. M/F: 99/1.

A.k.a. "TRAX"sational (as it says on its awning). This is the only gay bar in the upper Haight. Why they want to be in the Haight is more bewildering than why there are not more gay bars in the Haight. There is a lovely and somewhat safer view of Haight Street riff-raff from inside the bar. Occasionally breeders wander in who don't know this is a queer bar. Drab, dull gray-brown art deco interior. One pool table and a couple pinball machines. We suggest that whenever you find yourself trapped in the upper Haight, this might be a nice respite from panhandling, four-hundred-dollar-skateboard-owning, multi-pierced, I'm-white-but-I'm-trying-to-grow-dreadlocks-anyway freaks.

Wild Side West

424 Cortland at Wool. Neighborhood: Bernal Heights. Map: pg. 157. Phone: (415) 647-3099. Hours: 1 p.m. to 2 a.m. M/F: 30/70.

See Lesbians & Dykes; Bars, Clubs and Hangouts, page 113.

Cafés & Restaurants

These eating establishments are just a few favorites of Betty and Pansy and their friends. Please call the number listed to check the hours.

B R U N C H

Aunt Mary's

3122 16th St. at Valencia. Neighborhood: Mission. Map: pg. 176.
Phone: (415) 626-5523.

This is a funky breakfast spot. The cheesy decor is unintentional. The crowd consists of a weird mix of queer punks and entire Latino families just back from church. The food is inexpensive and yummy. This friendly family-owned restaurant closes quite early in the afternoon.

Café Flore

2298 Market at Noe. Neighborhood: Castro. Map: pg. 160. Phone: (415) 621-8579.

A.k.a. Café Hairdo, Café Attitude, Café Whore, et al. This is still one of the most popular and queer cafés in all of San Francisco. They have a counter to order California cuisine, which is usually tasty yet overpriced. The most desired table is in the left-hand corner as you walk in from the Market Street entrance. It is the only place to hold court. Good luck trying to find a seat outside on the weekend. The bench and line of tables that face Market Street are often referred to as "death row" as no one wants to sit there. By day the crowd is almost all queer. At night it is mostly clueless gays and het hipsters.

Cove Café

434 Castro near Market. Neighborhood: Castro. Map: pg. 160.
Phone: (415) 626-0462.

Betty says try the eggs benedict with french fries. See the lengthy description under Queer Favorites, page 70.

Dottie's True Blue Café

522 Jones at Geary. Neighborhood: Tenderloin. Map: pg. 170.
Phone: (415) 885-2767.

A great place for brunch if you're stuck in the Tenderloin, or even if you have to drive to get there. Eggs, pancakes and good standard brunch foods. Only open until 2 p.m. and closed on Tuesdays.

Just For You

*1453 18th St. at Connecticut. Neighborhood: Potrero Hill. Map: pg. 157.
Phone: (415) 647-3033.*

This groovy Potrero Hill eatery is dyke-owned and -operated. It is a great place to find and watch dykes. A few nice straight boys work here. The food is yummy, inexpensive and about four notches up from greasy spoon. You get to see them cook your meal as the space is tiny—a couple of tables and a long counter. We recommend the breakfast burrito and the fried potatoes. Just For You is an excellent dyke breakfast bet.

Patio Café

*531 Castro near 18th St. Neighborhood: Castro. Map: pg. 160.
Phone: (415) 621-4640.*

This place is huge and absolutely packed for weekend brunch. Breakfast and brunch are served daily from 8 a.m. to 4:45 p.m. It has a pieced-together atmosphere truly original to San Francisco. Waitrons are mostly young cute queer boys who never have a waist size larger than thirty inches. The clientele are mostly lesbians and gay men in their thirties and forties. Not a place to go on a rainy day, it is perfect however on sunny days as they open the roof.

Spaghetti Western

*576 Haight at Steiner. Neighborhood: The Haight. Map: pg. 164.
Phone: (415) 864-8461.*

If Georgia O'Keefe had been born thirty years later, lived in the lower Haight, been a major dyke and decided to open a restaurant that served white trash food, this would be it. It is totally surreal. The food is great also. Betty recommends their biscuits and sausage gravy.

Ti Couz Crêperie

*3108 16th St. at Valencia. Neighborhood: Mission. Map: pg. 176.
Phone: (415) 252-7373.*

This nifty crêperie has a medium price range. They offer breakfast, dessert, vegetarian and dinner crepes. Though queers gravitate here, it is often filled with straight folks.

CAFES

Café Macondo

3159 16th St. at Valencia. Neighborhood: Mission. Map: pg. 176.
Phone: (415) 863-6517.

This café, close to the Roxie Theater, is a great option if you want to be alone, study or chat quietly with a friend. Patrons are often discussing their relationships, the revolution, or playing chess. You can actually read a book here or write in your journal.

Cup-A-Joe

3801 17th St. at Sanchez. Neighborhood: Castro. Map: pg. 160.
Phone: (415) 487-1661.

This is the newest café in the Castro—but off the beaten path. Queers and funky straight folk mingle with ease here.

Jumpin' Java

139 Noe bet. Henry and 14th St. Neighborhood: Castro. Map: pg. 160.
Phone: (415) 431-5282. Hours: 7 a.m. to 10 p.m. every day.

This café came out of nowhere and is now a popular meeting place for all kinds of people. Right down the street from Café Flore, Jumpin' Java attracts a quieter, more studious crowd although there is still cruising action. The coffee is a high-octane brew, not for the faint of heart. This is one of the places where Pansy goes to get away from it all. The chai tea is a special favorite. They serve a variety of pastries but no substantial food. The staff is the most datable of any staff (meaning available, good-looking and willing). Features include the SF Net (computer on-line service), revolving art shows (some good, some bad) and a bulletin board.

Just Desserts

248 Church near Market. Neighborhood: Castro. Map: pg. 160.
Phone: (415) 626-5774.

Just Desserts is a San Francisco institution. Medium in size, with a lovely garden patio, this is the place to congregate at night. It is packed on the weekends, especially around 9 or 10 p.m. The staff is friendly, the music is always enjoyable, and the food is wonderful. One of the best selections of sweets and coffee in the country. The best poppy-seed cake this side of the galaxy. Definitely not the place for a diet. They will write anything on any cake you desire. The crowd ranges from grunge boys to very hetero yuppies. It is also one of the main hangouts for cool sober kids. Look for them in the back, smoking, laughing and throwing tea bags at the brick walls. Be sure to ask for Mistress Hiroko.

Mad Magda's Russian Tea Room

579 Hayes near Octavia. Neighborhood: Hayes Valley. Map: pg. 165.
Phone: (415) 864-7654.

This is the greatest café in all of Hayes Valley. It gets quite twisted at times. They have lots of forty-five rpm's, and the music is eclectic. For something a little different, try this joint.

The Orbit Room Café

1900 Market at Herman and Guerrero. Neighborhood: Upper Market. Map: pg. 160.
Phone: (415) 252-9525.

This Upper Market Street café has an extremely classy interior. They play good music, have a view of the intersection, and serve alcohol as well as food. The crowd consists of twenty-something straight kids and some queers.

Pasqua

4094 18th St. near Castro. Neighborhood: Castro. Map: pg. 160.
Phone: (415) 626-6263.

Let's face it—it's a chain but we love it. Pasqua is the quieter, attitude-free, non-smoking, more mature alternative to the Flore (see Brunch, page 58). On the weekend days, this place is packed inside and out. Some of the gay boys have taken to getting a parking spot early in front so they can sunbathe on the hoods. It also attracts a frighteningly large crowd of dog-walkers. Try not to step on the poor rascals who are always tied to the parking meters outside. What makes this spot so wonderful is the adorable staff. They are known for their quick wit and sexy ways. A friend of Betty's once ordered a small decaf latté with low-fat milk. The undaunted comic behind the counter screamed, "One 'why bother'?"

Red Dora's Bearded Lady Café and Gallery

485 14th St. at Guerrero. Neighborhood: Mission. Map: pg. 176.
Phone: (415) 626-2805.

See Lesbians & Dykes; Bars, Clubs and Hangouts, page 113
for information.

Spike's

4117 19th St. at Castro. Neighborhood: Castro. Map: pg. 160.
Phone: (415) 626-5573.

If you want to boycott corporate coffee in the Castro, Spike's
is your option for good coffee. They have a variety of fresh
coffees, teas and a huge selection of candy. Very casual, it is
amazingly quiet and peaceful. Regulars are often local mer-
chants on break from their busy day who do not want to deal
with unruly crowds. Extremely friendly and soft-spoken, the
staff donate all their tips to the AIDS Emergency Fund. If you
are lucky, you might even meet and get to pet Spike himself
who can occasionally be found sitting out front.

OPEN AFTER 2 AM

All Star Donuts

399 5th St. at Harrison. Neighborhood: SOMA. Map: pg. 174.
Phone: (415) 882-0889. Hours: 24/7.

Why do all the All Star Donuts have Chinese food, donuts
and lottery tickets? What's that all about? They also have the
best veggie burgers (after Hot 'n' Hunky). Conveniently
located near some of the lurkier spots south of Market (i.e.
Blow Buddies, City Entertainment, Folsom Gulch), this is a
great place to stuff yourself on pastries and coffee. Not a
good place to go if you are on chemicals or itching for trouble as it is a favorite hangout of the S.F.P.D. (like most donuts
shops).

Baghdad Café

2295 Market at 16th St. Neighborhood: Castro. Map: pg. 160.
Phone: (415) 621-4434. Hours: 24/7.

A.k.a. Bad Hag and Fag Dad. Baghdad is open twenty-four
hours and is probably the most popular twenty-four-hour

diner in the city. The employees are very cool, total babes, and usually very saucy. The food is not bad but recently became over-priced. Still, the space is clean and well-lit, and they don't kick you out as long as you order something. In fact, you can get away with hours of card playing here. This restaurant also offers a great view of the most dangerous intersection in the world, free of charge. There is a line every night at 1:45 a.m.

Clown Alley

42 Columbus at Jackson. Neighborhood: North Beach/Financial District. Map: pg. 157. Phone: (415) 421-2540. Hours: Fri and Sat until 2:40 a.m.

If you leave the bar or club of your choice a little early, you can stop by Clown Alley. Do not confuse it with the one on Lombard that closed. They offer typical diner fare (i.e. hot dogs and hamburgers) but have veggie offerings as well (i.e. eggplant sandwiches and garden burgers).

Denny's

1700 Post bet. Laguna and Webster. Neighborhood: Japantown. Map: pg. 165. Phone: (415) 563-1400. Hours: 24/7.

It is the old stand-by in most cities. I once realized several moments into a date that I did not want to be dating this particular fellow. When he said I could pick the restaurant, I chose Denny's hoping that would immediately turn him off. My excuse was that it was close to Kabuki where we were going to the movies. I also demanded a smoking section (when they still had one) much to his surprise. They no longer offer the free dinner on your birthday so go elsewhere to celebrate. The staff can be a bit uptight as well. A friend of mine was once thrown out because the Denny's folks felt that the rip in his jeans was a little too close to an obscene area of his body. Jeez strict. Plus let's not forget the major discrimination suits making national news around the country. But hey, if you're jonesing for some meatloaf, here is an option.

Grubstake

1525 Pine bet. Polk and Van Ness. Neighborhood: Polk. Map: pg. 168. Phone: (415) 673-8268.
Hours: Mon thru Fri 5 p.m. to 4 a.m., Sat and Sun 10 a.m. to 4 a.m.

A sure bet after visiting Polk Street bars. This small restaurant is housed inside an old railroad car. A dear friend and I **63** once arrived quite famished after a few too many at the Q.T. II. When our waiter arrived, my friend said she would like two orders of the half chicken. Without batting an eyelash, our waiter asked if she wanted mashed potatoes or fries with that. He was less than pleased when I tried to explain that it was a joke: two halves of a chicken is a *whole* chicken. I think it only seemed funny to us due to the liquor. You had to be there. Be nicer to the staff than we were; remember they have to deal with the Polk Street crowd a lot.

Happy Donuts

3801 24th St. at Church. Neighborhood: Noe Valley. Map: pg. 157.
Phone: (415) 285-5890. Hours: 24/7.

Yet another place to munch on a fatty donut. Keep your eyes peeled though as this was the location of the alleged attack by one of San Francisco's finest on his girlfriend. My question: Did the attack happen pre- or post-donut?

International House of Pancakes

2299 Lombard at Pierce. Neighborhood: Marina. Map: pg. 165.
Phone: (415) 921-4004. Hours: 24/7.

Why oh why must one of my favorite spots be all the way to hell over in the Marina of all places? Breakfast 24/7—pancakes, waffles, bad coffee, cute waitron uniforms and a scary variety of syrup. The blueberry dessert crepes rule this world. This is the IHOP location where Naomi witnessed a girl gang fight on New Year's Eve. Marina chicks and Sistas were bitch slapping each other while all wearing LBDs (little black dresses).

International House of Pancakes

825 Mission at 5th St. Neighborhood: SOMA. Map: pg. 174.
Phone: (415) 896-2401. Hours: 24/7.

This new IHOP is located directly underneath the club named Big Heart City (where gay clubs sometimes happen). In fact, they share the same front door. IHOP pipes in muzak for no apparent reason since the disco beat from upstairs overpowers any instrumental version of a Barry Manilow song. Imagine Christopher Cross singing back up for Rozalla. Who needs a smoking section when disco fog rolls down the staircase and delicately settles on your breakfast crepes? Our friend Naomi was particularly taken with the host who couldn't be interrupted while he recited his IHOP spiel (i.e. Hi, welcome to IHOP, how many in your party?) without having to start over from the beginning.

Jack-In-The-Box

366 Bayshore at Cortland. Neighborhood: near Bernal Heights. Map: pg. 157.
Phone: (415) 641-8467. Hours: 24/7.

If you really want fast food late at night, then this is the answer. The restaurant is not open twenty-four hours but the drive-thru is. Sourdough bacon cheeseburger and patty melts are the way to top an evening of merriment.

Jack-In-The-Box

400 Geary at Mason. Neighborhood: Union Square. Map: pg. 171.
Phone: (415) 673-0868. Hours: 24/7.

At some point in the evening, the dining room closes. However, if you want to stand, there is a small bar. Get it to go. Sourdough bacon cheeseburgers have saved Betty's life.

King Diner

1390 Mission at 10th St. Neighborhood: SOMA. Map: pg. 174.
Phone: (412) 552-2707. Hours: 24/7.

This diner is very popular with the very young straight kids. Passing the crowd outside on the sidewalk is often so scary I have never ventured inside. If you are a chickenhawk, have taken model mugging, or are an inner-city high school teacher, this might do the trick for your late night hunger pangs.

Lucky Penny

2670 Geary at Masonic. Neighborhood: Richmond. Map: pg. 164.
Phone: (415) 921-0836. Hours: 24/7.

This is the funkiest restaurant going—where to go to get out of the Castro on those days when you've seen enough gayness to stun an ox. There are amazingly hideous pictures (which are a laugh riot) on the menu. Late at night, be careful not to get caught up in any Asian gang dramas. If you love long, super-caffeinated chats with friends in cheesy diners, this is the place for you.

Mel's Drive-In

3355 Geary bet. Stanyan and Masonic. Neighborhood: Richmond. Map: pg. 164. Phone: (415) 387-2255. Hours: Sun thru Thurs 6 a.m. to 1 a.m., Fri and Sat 6 a.m. to 3 a.m.

A diner that serves classic diner food of yesteryear in a decor from the same period. Mel's is well-known as a site used in the filming of *American Graffiti*. The food and service are good, the interior is amazing, and it is one of the most spotless restaurants I have ever experienced. A great option for a date.

Mel's Drive-In

2165 Lombard bet. Fillmore and Steiner. Neighborhood: Marina. Map: pg. 165. Phone: (415) 921-2867. Hours: Sun thru Thurs til 2 a.m., Fri and Sat 24 hours.

See previous entry for details.

Mr. Pizza Man

2680 22nd St. at York. Neighborhood: Potrero Hill. Map: pg. 157. Phone: (415) 285-3337. Hours: 24/7.

Mr. Pizza Man's many locations throughout San Francisco deliver pizza, calzone, pasta, poultry, meats, seafood, salads, beer and wine twenty-four hours a day, seven days a week. If you would rather visit the restaurant, this location offers late-night hours.

Mr. Pizza Man

3409 Geary at Stanyan. Neighborhood: Richmond. Map: pg. 164. Phone: (415) 387-3131. Hours: til 4 or 5 a.m.

See above for details. This location has late-night eat-in hours as well.

North Beach Pizza

1499 Grant at Union. Neighborhood: North Beach. Map: pg. 157. Phone: (415) 433-2444. Hours: Sun thru Thurs 11 a.m. to 1 a.m., Fri and Sat 11 a.m. to 3 a.m.

If you want to go Italian, you might as well go to North Beach. Better yet, avoid the aging beatniks in the neighborhood by having your order delivered. We think it's the best pizza in the city.

Pizza Love

1245 Folsom bet. 8th and 9th Sts. Neighborhood: SOMA. Map: pg. 174.
Phone: (415) 252-1111. Hours: Sun, Mon, Tues, Wed til midnight; Thurs til 2 a.m.;
Fri and Sat til 4 a.m

This pizza joint is right in the middle of the Folsom strip of gay bars. Calzone, pastas, sandwiches and a salad bar are available as well. Although they have lots of seating and a friendly staff, they also offer free delivery including beer and wine. While you are waiting for your order, you can occupy yourself with pinball machines, video games and a pool table. Note: The help has a nasty habit of sneezing, coughing and taking grubby money without washing their hands. Please remind them to wash before handling your food.

Rolling Pin

497 Castro at 18th St. Neighborhood: Castro. Map: pg. 160.
Phone: (415) 431-6112. Hours: 24/7.

If you like adventurous late-night snacks, the Castro's Rolling Pin, a favorite hangout of homeless folks, stray freaks and drunk queens, is a good bet. The brave and/or stupid eat in. The timid and/or enlightened get it to go. As a resident, it is important to have at least one Rolling Pin horror story. Besides donuts, these folks also offer steamed hot dogs, which are hard to find in this town.

Rolling Pin

2401 California at Fillmore. Neighborhood: Fillmore. Map: pg. 165.
Phone: (415) 931-0817. Hours: 24/7.

See above for details.

Sparky's

242 Church at Market. Neighborhood: Upper Market. Map: pg. 160.
Phone: (415) 621-6001. Hours: 24/7.

The crowd seems to consist of straight hipsters and queer people in their twenties and thirties. The staff work their butts off and are often quite attractive. This place is pervaded by a strange neon-like aura that always makes Betty feel like she is in some sort of dream state. Several times, she has almost gotten into fights with assaholic straight men in line for the bathroom. The first night she ever went to Sparky's also happened to be her first acid trip and New Year's Eve, which left a lasting impression. It seems that many have visited this place while on acid. In fact, one night, Bob, David and Troy were headed for Uranus when they were verbally taunted by rabid homophobes in a car. They responded by kicking and denting the new car. Spotting cops nearby, they slipped into Uranus and dropped a tab. Unfortunately, the cops followed, arrested and held them in prison for several hours. When they were released, all they wanted was a diner that played Madonna songs. They arrived at Sparky's to hear just that—the entire Madonna tape in fact. What's the significance? I don't know. Note: When going to the bathroom, never, we repeat, *never* turn around and glance into the kitchen. Don't Ask. Don't Tell. Don't Look.

Taquerias

Taquerias are located along Mission St. bet. 16th and 24th Sts. Map: pg. 176.

Some stay open late or all night. However, the haphazard hours of operation are constantly in flux. If you are itching for a burrito, take a stroll in this neighborhood and you will find at least one place offering true Mexican fare.

Zim's

3490 California at Locust. Neighborhood: Pacific Heights. Map: pg. 165.
Phone: (415) 775-6699. Hours: 24/7.

This twenty-four-hour-a-day option is never really one's preference as much as one's only option. Betty once received a magnetic knife with her late-night breakfast. All the other silverware stuck to it. Her friends encouraged her to steal it, but she was afraid that the cost of the knife might be removed from the pay of the nine-months pregnant waitress.

2223 Market St.

2223 Market at Sanchez. Neighborhood: Castro. Map: pg. 160.
Phone: (415) 431-0692.

A.k.a. No Name on Market because they have not named it yet. When they answer the phone they refer to themselves by their address, thus their listing. The food is wonderful— from homemade handmade pizzas to shrimp and pasta. The filet mignon special is the best filet mignon you'll ever have. Best burgers in town for lunch. Pricey but not over the top. They have no problems with special orders. A wonderful wine list and after-dinner drink list. If you want dinner, call for reservations as there is always a wait because the food is just that good. Waiters are casual, professional and friendly. Good service without attitude. Atmosphere is loud but you can still hold a conversation.

Bad Man José's

4077 18th St. near Castro. Neighborhood: Castro. Map: pg. 160.
Phone: (415) 861-1706.

Bad Man's nachos are the tastiest item. Get them to go: there is never enough space to sit down, or you have to sit centimeters from queens in a bitch fight. Betty is afraid to sit at the counter because she is sure that during an earthquake one of the super humongous masks on the wall will fall off and kill her.

Café Luna Piena

558 Castro near 18th St. Neighborhood: Castro. Map: pg. 160.
Phone: (415) 621-2566.

This restaurant recently opened in the space that used to be the Castro Gardens. The new owners were shocked and horrified when they realized that the kitchen consisted entirely of a bank of microwave ovens! After extensive renovation, they opened Luna Piena, which has been serving excellent, reasonably priced Italian food, with inconsistent service. The Caesar salad is a particular favorite. The back deck is gorgeous and a wonderful spot by day or evening. It's a good place to take a date, or your parents.

Unfortunately, our resident Luna Piena expert says that John the fabulous chef just left, and she can't vouch for the food. In fact, based on what she ate the last time she was there, they may have gone back to those microwaves! Since it was definitely the food and not the service that kept people going back, we wonder what will happen. The Castro needs more good, affordable restaurants, so we hope that the owners work out their problems and get another good chef in there.

Cove Café

434 Castro near Market. Neighborhood: Castro. Map: pg. 160.
Phone: (415) 626-0462.

For over nine years, Pansy has been eating here, where she always feels as though she is at her favorite grandmother's. The space is clean and very well lit. The waitrons are always fast, courteous and friendly. Betty and Pansy love them all: Derrick, Annie, and that nasty Irish boy Noel (who loves '70s music just like Betty). The food is fresh and homemade. Recently Pansy and Scott O'Hara went there for lunch, prompting one waiter to remark, "Oh my god, it's a celebrity luncheon." Pansy and Scott schmoozed while Solange kept the groveling masses at bay. Betty recommends the meatloaf. Do not miss the gorgeous portrait of your esteemed authors hanging on the wall.

Hamburger Mary's

1582 Folsom at 12th St. Neighborhood: SOMA. Map: pg. 174.
Phone: (415) 626-1985. Hours: Sun thru Thurs til 1 a.m., Fri and Sat til 2 a.m.

This hamburger joint, with great pinball machines, is populated by the hip and trendy—gay or straight. It is not as queer as it used to be. The kitsch on the walls (including drag queens) is quite delightful but the smut element that made the decor one-of-a-kind was toned down long ago. They have of late been employing a very flirty bus staff. Be sure to ask for Jack. Rumor has it he was a Mapplethorpe model.

Hot 'n' Hunky

4039 18th St. near Hartford. Neighborhood: Castro. Map: pg. 160.
Phone: (415) 621-6365.

HNH has the best hamburgers and chocolate shakes in the whole damn world. Betty recommends the garden burger, patty o' melt, or chicken in a basket. The jukebox selections rule. Bow down and kiss the feet of Scott the HNH God. Chiquita has been working here longer than most folks have lived in San Francisco. The other staff members are living dolls as well. B&P demand that you tip them well. This is the only surviving branch of the HNH chain. The other branches that went under obviously did not have Scott at the helm. If this one goes under, B&P will starve to death.

Josie's Juice Joint and Cabaret

3583 16th St. at Market. Neighborhood: Castro. Map: pg. 160.
Phone: (415) 861-7933.

By day this is a vegetarian restaurant and café. At night it is transformed into the hottest queer cabaret this side of the Greenwich Time Line. Folks come here for a quiet breakfast, brunch or lunch. The food is great and reasonably priced. You can eat inside or enjoy the lovely outdoor area. See also Things Not to Miss, page 139.

La Mediterranée

288 Noe near Market. Neighborhood: Castro. Map: pg. 160.
Phone: (415) 431-7210.

This is Betty's top all-around pick. The food is amazingly delicious and surprisingly inexpensive. Betty recommends the filo-dough combination plate. The atmosphere is comfy. The service is fast and friendly; the waitresses are always cool. During the day you can sit at one of the two tables on the sidewalk. The only upsetting thing is that it is closed on Mondays.

New Dawn Café

3174 16th St. near Guerrero. Neighborhood: Mission. Map: pg. 176.
Phone: (415) 553-8888.

The interior is trashy, eclectic punk rock. The food, served in gigantic portions, is pretty good all around. The home fries are excellent. On weekends it can get pretty crowded, especially for breakfast (served all day), but the wait should not be that long since the restaurant is good-sized. Order your food at the counter from a friendly yet disinterested mod prim, and take a seat at one of the great formica tables. There is plenty to look at while you wait.

Pozole

2337 Market at Noe. Neighborhood: Castro. Map: pg. 160. Phone: (415) 626-2666.

Land of the chesty waiters. Pozole must be the segue from the Third World to runway modeling for gorgeous men. The service is really good. The molé (chicken or beef made with a orange/raw chocolate sauce) seems overpriced for burritos and papusa (Salvadoran food) but you do get what you pay for. They serve a variety of low-fat items for the health conscious and a unique selection of burritos you would not find at a taqueria. The atmosphere is filled with authentic music, art and religious imagery.

Thai House Bar & Café

2200 Market at Sanchez and 15th St. Neighborhood: Castro. Map: pg. 160. Phone: (415) 864-5006.

This is Betty's favorite Thai restaurant. Their Pad Thai is the best anywhere. Order a Thai iced coffee. Their prices are inexpensive and the service is great. You generally do not have to wait long for a table. The interior is clean, well-lit and comfortable. The whole place is filled with dykes and fags on dates. If it's too crowded, you can always go to the other Thai House (same owners) around the corner on Noe Street.

Welcome Home

464 Castro bet. Market and 18th St. Neighborhood: Castro. Map: pg. 160. Phone: (415) 626-3600.

The name says it all. Here you will eat home-style cooking without attitude. The iced tea is served in giant plastic glasses just like Mom used to have. They also feature excellent homemade desserts. Breakfast is served all day, and the specials change daily. The service, of course, is friendly. Welcome Home is a great place to eat regular old food in the Castro.

Zuni Café

1658 Market. Neighborhood: Upper Market. Map: pg. 160. Phone: (415) 552-2522.

With its pleasing Southwest decor, gracious staff and acute sense of culinary precision, this airy eatery has set the pace for fabulous California cuisine for over fifteen years. Sure, the weekend wait, even with a reservation, can be gruesome. But that gives you all the more time to lean on the lovely copper bar, taste-test the oyster menu and quaff any one of the thirteen domestic and international beers. If you get past the door staff, Table 1 is the power table, Table 8 is the place to do business, Table 12 and 14 (see and be seen) are our favorites, Table 51 and 52 for brunch, Table 71—the date table. Sample the extensive, sommelier-produced wine and champagne list (including Veuve Clicquot by the glass). While you're at it, check out the pretty yuppie-meets-art-fag crowd. Ad execs, Silicon Valley swells, policy wonks, multi-media gurus, entertainers, politicos, CEOs—all converge for the rotating menu, which also boasts standards like the amazing chicken (yes, it really takes forty-five minutes to prepare), creamy-dreamy polenta, palate-pleasing salads, astonishing fish dishes, and what some consider to be the best burger in town. Don't believe us? Then ask recent diners, who've included Mick Jagger and Jerry Hall, Brad Pitt, Richard Gere and Cindy Crawford (the chicken alone kept them together a few extra months), Bill Gates, Robin Williams, Alice Walker, Tracy Chapman, Danny Glover, Nicholas Cage, Neil Young, Ted Kennedy, George Stephanopolous, porn star Jason Andrews, Rickie Lee Jones, Carol Burnett, Fran Liebowitz, Jackson Browne, Boz Scaggs, George Lucas, David Hockney, and former Texas Governor Ann Richards. Not that we need to drop names to convince you that, with its spare but comfy environs and its consistently laid back approach to casually elegant dining, the sleek and chic Zuni Café proves once and for all that, for standard-bearing restaurants, fussy is *finished*.

Most clubs in San Francisco are fly-by-night operations. For this reason, we *implore* you to call the phone number if one is listed. Verify that the club is still in operation before you get all gussied up and arrive on the doorstep to discover it's closed—or worse yet—it's straight night.

Unlike bars, clubs usually operate one night a week. They are listed below on the night that they are known to be open; pay attention to the heading so you don't show up on the wrong day. We have narrowed our list of queer clubs to the ones that have been around for over a year. We suggest you check the weekly gay papers for evidence that they still exist. There are two free bi-weekly papers that offer current clubs listings: *Odyssey,* with its "Jet Boy" and "Jet Girl" sections, and *Oblivion*.

T U E S D A Y

Breathe Deep

1015 Folsom at 6th St. Neighborhood: SOMA. Map: pg. 174. Phone: DNA. Hours: 11 p.m. to 4:30 a.m. Cover: $5.00. M/F: 75/25.

This small club is like a younger cousin to Lift (see Thursday, page 77) and attracts a similar crowd. Resident DJ Ruben Mancias is building himself a good reputation and a small following among house-heads. Strong gay presence, but not a gay club per se. This is a late-night event where people seem to drift in slowly between 12:30 and 2 a.m. If only we did not have to work in the mornings.

W E D N E S D A Y

Baby Judy's

527 Valencia near 16th St. (Casanova Bar). Neighborhood: Mission. Map: pg. 176. Phone: DNA. Hours: 10 p.m. to 2 a.m. Cover: $3.00. M/F: 60/40.

The DJs are the always delightful Deena Davenport and Alvin A Go-Go. The musical selections include new wave, disco, grunge, hip-hop, muzak, punk, show tunes, go-go, synthe-pop and funk. The always fun funny funky weirdo crowd makes even us twenty-somethings feel ancient. Cracked Out Ho' refers to Baby Judy's as the cast party for the film *Kids.* An extremely social atmosphere full of chatty Cathys, but folks still dance and cruise. This spot is filled with the hottest young boys of any venue these days. They serve lots of great beer for $3.00 a pint. There is little ventilation though, so prepare to sweat.

T H U R S D A Y

The Box

715 Harrison at 3rd St. Neighborhood: SOMA. Map: pg. 174.
Phone: (415) 647-8258. Hours: 9 p.m. to 2 a.m. Cover: $6.00. M/F: 75/25.

The oldest running club in San Francisco, The Box has been happening for over seven years and is still very popular. If a club lasts a year in San Francisco, it is considered a success. Different from other clubs, the majority of the crowd comes here for one thing: DANCING. It is also one of the most racially diverse crowds of any club in the city.

In March of 1994, when The Box moved from its previous space on Divisadero, folks were nervous that the club might lose its touch, but it appears as busy and popular as ever. The new space has lots of lurky, maze-like balcony areas. Of the two bars, the larger one downstairs—in the same room as the small dance floor which plays funky music from the past and present—is always crowded. The crowd here has a great time, and they love the music. The upstairs bar is located in a more secluded lounge area with a large, circular, red velvet sofa, which is very comfy. Here, there is rarely a line to get a drink. There is also a small beanbag room. You can view the main dance floor from this lounge. Despite the lounge and balconies, the main dance floor is where it all happens at The Box. These aren't club kids; they are people who like to dance sober. The music varies from pretty typical club music to retro hits. It's obvious that some people live for this club; others merely show up to bask in the energy and sweat.

Lift

55 Natoma bet. 1st and 2nd Sts. and Mission and Howard. Neighborhood: SOMA.
Map: pg. 174. Phone: (415) 267-5984. Hours: 11:30 p.m. to 5:30 a.m.
M/F: 70/30. Cover: $5.00.

Lift is a late-night club with New York City style. The music, usually deep and underground house, is completely fierce. Features DJs like David Harness, Aaron O., jamie j and Ruben Mancias. An attractive twenty-something crowd mixes gay/straight, boy/girl, white/black/Latin/Asian. These folks are house music aficionados, and they come to dance (but usually not much else). Don thy baggy apparel. Several rooms off the main dance floor offer lounging, pool or pinball; and a second dance area provides a slower groove of funky hip-hop or dance-hall reggae. Most people arrive around 2 a.m. Lots of folks walk or cab it over here after kickin' it at The Box.

FRIDAY

Asia

174 King at 3rd St. Neighborhood: SOMA. Map: pg. 174. Phone: DNA. Hours: 10 p.m. until after-hours. M/F: 90/10. Cover: $10.00.

This place is sort of like the N' Touch bar, but bigger and just a little more hip. The music improved noticeably when they enlisted jamie j to work the turntable. Loads of hot Asian men and boys. The crowd is fun, and the bar staff is pretty friendly (say hi to Hunter). The go-go boys are cute, but so far only one has been Asian. Relax on the balcony to drink it all in, or work the tearoom.

SATURDAY

177 Townsend

177 Townsend at 3rd St. Bar: Townsend. Neighborhood: SOMA. Map: pg. 174.

Popular with folks who like large dance floors, this is the largest club in the city: a huge warehouse with a large circular bar, large stage and huge bathrooms. Plus, an incredible all-new light show. A variety of clubs occupy either one of its two addresses: 177 Townsend or 174 King Street. Straight and gay happenings occur here but the straight happenings are few and far between. The bartenders are friendly and fun and gorgeous. Don't mess with security—they are scary and mean business (i.e. don't try to have sex in the bathroom). Also, though Ms. Betty has seen (but certainly never used) drugs here, you do not want to get caught. They will confiscate the drugs though normally they do not eighty-six you. Don't share anything with anyone in a bathroom stall as Betty once saw two drag queens eating oreos and talking shop when they got busted. Saturday night is the night: it has a larger variety of folks from the electrolysis, steroid and crystal crowd to the club kids with platform Converses. Sunday is more to draw in the T-shirt and blue jeans casual and not the fashion-and-body-conscious crowd. A variety of DJs but they all play house (not doctor). Decorations change every week. Smart bar available for the health conscious or recently detoxed.

Club Futura

174 King at 3rd St. Neighborhood: SOMA. Map: pg. 174. Phone: ???.
Hours: alternating Sat 10 p.m. to after-hours. Cover: $10.00. M/F: 90/10.

Caters to a gay Latino crowd. The music ranges from banda and Mexican pop to Latin house. We wish they would play more salsa. The boys are cute—*muy caliente,* even—but there's a lot more of them when something special is planned for that week. This occurs in the same space as Club Asia (see Friday, page 78) and usually the night after, so pick your flavor carefully. The clubbier people end up later at Club Universe, around the corner.

GirlSpot

278 11th St. at Folsom (VSF). Neighborhood: SOMA. Map: pg. 174.
Phone: (415) 337-4962. Hours: 8 p.m. to 2 a.m. Cover: $6.00 after 10 p.m., less before 10 p.m. M/F: 7/93.

See Lesbians & Dykes; Bars, Clubs and Hangouts (page 110) for more information.

S U N D A Y

401 6th at Harrison (The EndUp)

401 6th St. at Harrison. Neighborhood: SOMA. Map: pg. 174. Phone: (415) 543-7700. Cover: $5.00. M/F: 75/25.

Cracked Out Ho' relates that the most accurate description of The EndUp he has heard is, "It's a place for people who have hit rock-bottom and decided to work with it." It's the perfect place to spend a Sunday morning, afternoon or evening because it is the biggest gathering of freaks in the city where trashiness is rewarded. Due to the low cover (no longer free) and the fact that there is basically nowhere else to go during the day, The EndUp draws a very "diverse" crowd. Everyone from drag queens to straight ravers to retail queens to those who have a hard time distinguishing fantasy from reality all dance, drink and talk together amiably. Many folks in attendance are either coming down, still up or revving up for more fun. Alcohol has become the surprising new drug of choice. There are fewer tweekers than in the past. The music is hit and miss—sometimes funky, sometimes techno, but usually danceable. Often, in the late afternoon and early evening, they play some of the best jazzy music in the city. Beware of the occasional free barbecue. You get what you pay for. For more details see Bars, SOMA, page 38.

Muffdive

527 Valencia at 16th St. (Casanova Bar). Neighborhood: Mission. Map: pg. 176. Phone: DNA. Hours: Sun nights only, 10 p.m. to 2 a.m. Cover: $3.00. M/F: 5/95.

See Lesbians & Dykes; Bars, Clubs and Hangouts (page 112) for info.

Pleasuredome

177 Townsend near 3rd St. Neighborhood: SOMA. Map: pg. 174. Phone: (415) 985-5256. Hours: 8 p.m. to 6 a.m. Cover: $5.00 - $7.00. M/F: 95/5.

This club makes folks hate Monday mornings. Sporadically the best club in SF. Lately, the music has been wonderful—great jazzy and trance music. The crowd usually consists of two very distinct groups: those with jobs and those with drugs. Of course, there is a gray area mixing jobs with drugs and not doing either in excess. The boys with jobs arrive fairly early around 10 p.m. and are usually on the way out by 2 a.m. The cracked-out crowd does not get there until around 1 a.m., and they don't leave until The EndUp reopens at 6 a.m. on Monday. So, for about an hour from 1 to 2 a.m., the dance floor is packed until the boys with jobs start going home. Then you are left with the cracked-out boys that you danced with on Saturday night and all day at The EndUp. Nevertheless, these cracked-out ho's are hot even when they look like they've been up for days, and they love dancing. The older muscle queen crowd of the past seems to have given up on Pleasuredome. Folks are friendly and enjoy the great space. Pleasuredome is the only place to be if there is a Monday holiday. They usually have to open up the back room to accommodate the crowd. The down side is that the humidity makes this place feel like a swamp.

G E N E R A L

MT Productions

584 Castro St., Suite #206 / San Francisco, CA 94114.
Phone: (415) 337-4962.

See Lesbians & Dykes; Bars, Clubs and Hangouts (page 111)
for info.

Under World

Phone: (415) 978-9448.

"One Thousand Boys in Briefs." It is what it sounds like—an
underwear party. You show up at the door, and they hand
you a garbage bag to put all of your clothes in except your
underwear and shoes. As the song goes, you can keep your
hat on. You can just imagine what kind of atmosphere hundreds of queer boys running around in nothing but their
underwear produces. There is usually a lurky area provided.
In recent times S.F.P.D. has been doing unannounced "random" visits to SOMA queer clubs and bars to card folks. The
cops hit this place and ended up arresting approximately four
of the guys and dragging them off in their underwear.
Allegedly for indecent exposure (they said that their penises
were visible). Who was complaining? Leave it to the S.F.P.D.
to sniff out an exposed penis or two or three. This is a
voyeur's delight, but keep your eyes peeled for the boys in
blue.

SPACES

The following spaces generally tend to host queer clubs. Just because a club occupies one of these spaces does not guarantee that it is queer or even queer friendly. Check *Odyssey* for a listing in the "Jet Boy" and "Jet Girl" sections, *Oblivion*, or ads in *B.A.R.*, *Frontiers* or *Bay Times*.

9th and Harrison/The Stud

399 9th St. at Harrison. Neighborhood: SOMA. Map: pg. 174.
Phone: (415) 863-6623. Hours: 5 p.m. to 2 a.m., sometimes to 3 a.m.
Cover: free to $3.00. M/F: 85/15.

This great space is the occasional host to a new or recently popular yet homeless club. It's wonderful no matter what day of the week. Wednesday nights are popular but Betty recommends Sunday nights. For more information see Bars, SOMA, page 44.

55 Natoma/540 Howard (DV8)

55 Natoma bet. 1st and 2nd Sts. and Mission and Howard. Neighborhood: SOMA. Map: pg. 174.

Club after club has lived and died in this space. Queer clubs don't seem to last as long here as straight ones. Perhaps it is those few extra blocks. Lift (see Thursday, page 77) is one of the longest survivors, but there is a sizable straight contingent. The space itself is fun with lots of little rooms to explore and hang out in. They charge for water.

174 King

174 King bet. 2nd and 3rd Sts. Neighborhood: SOMA. Map: pg. 174.

This space is located on the alley behind 177 Townsend. At times the doors are opened so folks can pass from one to the other. This is a small warehouse space, which should still be considered large by bar standards. It is extremely spartan and reminds one of a building refurbished to house a new outlet in a mall. There is a large balcony that wraps around and overlooks one end of the dance floor. It often hosts straight clubs and, on occasion, after-hours queer clubs that burn brightly and extinguish quickly.

177 Townsend

177 Townsend at 3rd St. Neighborhood: SOMA. Map: pg. 174.

A.k.a. Townsend. See Saturday, page 78.

401 6th at Harrison/The EndUp

401 6th St. at Harrison. Neighborhood: SOMA. Map: pg. 174.
Phone: (415) 543-7700.

This place is an institution. The outdoor deck is great. It opens at 6 a.m. on Saturday, Sunday and Monday mornings. Sunday is the best of the three. Monday is a bit depressing because you begin to wonder if these people have a home. The exception, however, is a Monday holiday, in which case it is even more fun than Sunday because it is a HOLIDAY. For more info see Bars, SOMA, page 38.

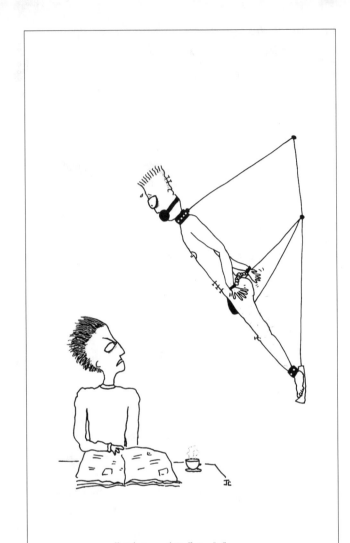

I thought I told you
to stop looking at me!

Cruising

This chapter gives you the low-down on places to cruise for sex with men—where you can skip the courting and cut to the action. Pick your favorite venue by checking out the headings: Outdoors, Sex Clubs, Tearooms, Theaters and Video Arcades.

OUTSIDE

If you are going cruising outside, remember the following safety tips: Bring a whistle; if you run into trouble, blow hard and run like hell. If you see someone being bashed, blow your whistle hard; and do what you can to kill the attacker until help arrives. Stay off the beaten path. By day there are folks who get horribly offended and make calls so don't tease or taunt the straight people by exposing yourself. When you are cruising outside at night, remember that it is preferable to go with friends, and carry your whistle. Let people know in advance where you are going, or write it on a scrap of paper so that the police can find it when you disappear. Wear your glasses. Stay sober. Bring the ever-convenient lighter or five-thousand-watt pen light.

Baker Beach

Ah, Baker Beach. Who can describe the wonder of this place? Pansy loves it on wet, rainy or foggy days. The first section of Baker Beach is largely het. Close to the cliffs it gets pretty mixed, and nude sun bathing occurs here frequently. Beyond the large rock formations, which are most easily navigated at low tide, the truly gay men's section begins to take shape. Pansy used to encounter humpy military boys from the Presidio at this beach but since the Army left town they are severely lacking. The cliffs can be treacherous though, so be careful. Sex goes on all over the beach and the cliffs, as well as on the many different levels of forest from the aforementioned rock formation all the way to the Golden Gate Bridge. Pansy also advises that you avoid swimming here because people have been dragged away and drowned by the undertow. It is the one public sex space where safe sex seems to be *de rigor,* which is a plus in Pansy's book. See you there. See map, page 156.

Buena Vista Park

Twenty-four hours a day, three hundred and sixty-five days a year, this locale has got it going on. As of late, the scene has been somewhat diminished by the Department of Parks and Recreation's obsessive-compulsive tree trimming and landscaping that more resembles the slash-and-burn technique in the South American rain forest. They claim that the clearing prevents soil erosion, which is like calling an

Intercontinental Ballistic Missile a peace keeper. The only way that they will ever get queens completely out of that park is to raze the hill, and that just won't happen. In the meantime, find little niches or carve them out (like a radiating species) and enjoy. The best times to go vary tremendously. The boys come in shifts: dog-walkers and local residents at sunset; a larger, and still sober crowd at 10 p.m.; the messy folks start showing up at 1 a.m. or so; and the scariest freaks show up at 3 or 4 a.m. By night the busiest area is the lookout flats at the top of the park on the extreme east side. By day the busiest area is on the hill to the south of the paved road. The northern slope is rarely used and is to be avoided. If the police cruise through with search lights, which is not common but happens, simply hit the ground as far away from the road as possible. Those donut connoisseurs would never pick their fat asses up out of the cruiser to scream at you.

Pansy once witnessed a fellow who discovered his prey in the shadow of the night and quickly began rimming him. After several moments it became obvious to Pansy and said rimmer that the rimmee was a homeless man without access to the Body Shop. It ruined a lovely moment for half a dozen horndogs. The lesson to learn is that you should look (squint, investigate, and beam your mag light) before you leap. The homeless do live here, nap here, and like us, some have sex here. See map, page 164.

Castro Theater Parking Lot

Pansy finds it best to meet someone on Castro Street (between 18th and Market Streets) and then take them to this dark spot. Tricks can be found in any of the numerous bars, not to mention A Different Light Bookstore. Having sex here is safest in a car or truck, unless you enjoy group scenes. Only a nighttime event, the best times are Friday and Saturday nights and after 2:30 a.m., as drunken queens are still trying to find their cars after the bars heave them out. This is extremely hit-or-miss and lately has been dull at best. Be aware that this spot is also peopled by homeless folks. See map, page 160.

Collingwood Park

This block in the Castro (18th, 19th, Collingwood and Diamond) is a.k.a. Eureka Valley Playground, The

87

Promenade, The Fruit Loop, The Sidewalk Sale, The Easter Parade, et al. The most activity (walking aimlessly) occurs between 2 a.m. and 6 a.m. There have been neighborhood meetings to discuss the problem of all the people and noise here at night. We are sympathetic to the neighbors' plight as we have seen screaming queens hanging out of sun roofs of circling cars and gaggles of chattering queens tanked to their tits who could not shut the hell up. Girls, if you don't mind your manners, this excellent space will be taken from us all. So be quiet, be courteous, don't litter, stay off private property, and for godsake keep cruising with the knowledge that others are trying to sleep. Collingwood seems pretty safe, but Betty's ex-roommate Cracked Out Ho' did lose a few dollars and a Fast Pass once. It was not because she dropped them. Don't trust anyone who won't get out of his car. There could be scary surprises in that car, not the least of which is probably a fat, hairy belly. People have been picked up here by seemingly queer guys, then bashed at another location. Cracked Out Ho' says that, at some point in the evening, a gallon of ice cream sounds like more fun than going home with a stranger. At this point, remember that CALA Foods is open twenty-four hours and on the same block that you are. See map, page 160.

Dolores Park

This scary park has gotten scarier, although there are fewer drug deals than before because more police are checking out the area. Supposedly someone was murdered here, but we can't substantiate the rumor. Pansy has seen youths with guns (one was a BB gun) but says she knows of lots of folk having good sex here anyway. Pansy was present one night when the cops rolled into each end of the park, and she had to make a run for it and tripped and cracked her rib (sue the S.F.P.D.). Not the park to go to if you are stupid or drunk. Always go with your friends or your family. Enter the park at the stairway on 19th and Church. Betty claims that 10 p.m. is a good time, but she would not dare enter this park until 2 a.m. when all straight people are asleep. All the action takes place under the walkover bridge near the MUNI tracks or along the sidewalk that is parallel to Church Street. This is definitely a nighttime space only. If anything seems amiss or if you are at all uncomfortable, your first priority is your safety. Better embarrassed than embalmed. This park is frequented by people from the neighborhoods it borders, Castro and Mission. Pansy once picked up a Marine (whose shirt read "Special Forces—Mess With the Best, Die Like the Rest"). They went to the corner of the park where the children's playground is located and the Marine begged Ms. Pansy to fuck him on the wooden structure. Betty has not returned to this park since one drug-addled eve when she was determined to squeeze blood from a turnip. When health conscious neighbors started jogging by with Labrador retrievers, Betty asked herself the reverberating question, "What am I doing here?" See map, page 160.

Dore Alley

This is one of the historic spots south of Market for men to get together and do it in a public space. These days it is hit-or-miss, mostly miss. Dore is located between Howard and Folsom and 9th and 10th Streets. This alley is largely a night space, except during the street fair. If you feel the need for alley action, we suggest Ringold and Shipley over this almost mythic location. See map, page 174.

Golden Gate Park

A.k.a. Queen Wilhemina's Tulip Path. This path runs the width of the west end of Golden Gate Park between the two windmills. If you have a car, drive to the west end of the park by the ocean. If you are arriving in the evening, you should park on Lincoln Drive to avoid a $55.00 parking ticket. If traveling on foot, you better jump on the 5 Fulton because it is a major hike. This path used to be lined with an assortment of paths and trails in the bushes beaten down by queens beating off. Recently the police are more present and the shrubbery is less present. New sex trails are being formed, however, and there seem to be many more youngsters. If you need an excuse to be here by day, borrow someone's dog.

The April 1993 issue of the *Richmond Review* carried an article on the front page, proclaiming "Gay 'Cruising' Called a Problem at Golden Gate Park." In the article, straight park goers complained of being propositioned, verbally harassed, and witness to gay sex. These concerned citizens referred to the area as both "virus village" and "weirdo trail." An anonymous source claimed that several gardeners were so disgusted that they asked to be transferred away from the west end of the park. Mounted and plain clothes officers have been patrolling this area. To punish queens, cops give tickets to folks who are not on "the one-and-only" main path. The highlight of the article is the twenty-three-year veteran tree-topping supervisor who claims it is not a problem and is the same situation as fifty years ago. He claims that the closure of the gay bathhouses forced men "out of the tubs and into the shrubs." Keep in mind that this is federal land and does not fall under the jurisdiction of S.F.P.D. Unsuspecting straight people do pass through here; try to avoid them. Our advice is to be aware of your surroundings. Do not taunt or flaunt near straight passersby. Cruise on the beaten path, and do your business off the beaten path, out of sight. Bashings have occurred at night. You are on the edge of the Pacific Ocean; you are not close to safety. This is not a gay friendly neighborhood but "gay" boys do go here to do the wild thing. Recently, Pansy was thrown to the ground by a youthful soccer player who sucked him dry, and Daviddog did it in a tree with some Bear. See map, page 158.

Lafayette Park

A.k.a. the Fairy Prairie. At almost any time of day, especially on weekends, one will find queens of all sizes, shapes and colors sunning on the hillside. A great place to meet men, it is totally hot sex in the forest atop the hill at night. Many prefer to grab a stud on nearby Polk Street and then go to Lafayette to get laid. See you there.

Cruise by day, fuck by night. Undercover police officers have been known to entrap folks in the bathrooms and bushes (our queer tax dollars at work). There have been arrests. Unfortunately for the S.F.P.D., many of the people arrested turned out to be straight (oops). See map, page 165.

Land's End

Once this was one of the last unpruned vestiges of man-to-man sex in the San Francisco wilderness. The area is large and inviting with a nice-sized beach and lots of play space. Some go about fully clothed, whilst others pretend to be Adam in Eden—before Eve came along. Scott O'Hara informs us that his visits of late have been fruitless. Folks are not cruising, paths are overgrown, and Parks and Rec people are handing out tickets to nudes for public lewdness (unless they are on the beach proper). Please visit during the day; this is dangerous terrain, and you might slip and fall by night. See map, page 156.

Ringold Alley

Ringold (pronounced Rhine gold—just like the stuff that got all the Germanic deities in trouble in the Wagnerian operas) is located between Folsom and Harrison and 8th and 9th Streets. A couple of years ago, a man was cruising this alley and was kidnapped by several guys in a van. They threw a blanket over him and drove him to another location where they took turns sodomizing him. They returned him to Ringold where they dumped him out. If you are going to continue to cruise despite anything anyone tells you, please consider taking model mugging and/or other self-defense classes. Please learn to cruise with good friends. See map, page 174.

Shipley Alley

This alley is located between Folsom and Howard and 5th and 6th Streets, directly behind Folsom Gulch (see Cruising, Video Arcades, page 102). It is always happening in the evening. Boys from the two nearby video-booth establishments stop by here. Those cars continuously cruising by are not residents looking for good parking. The best time is 3 a.m. when both of the video-booth establishments kick out the still-haven't-gotten-offs. See map, page 174.

SEX CLUBS

Generally sex clubs in San Francisco are places where you go to have sex with others. This is, of course, not mandatory. There are a variety to choose from, and the commitment ranges from paying admission and just walking around to handing over your apparel in a mandatory clothes check. Decide what you are most comfortable with, keeping in mind that almost everyone at these establishments is here for sex.

1808 Club

1808 Market at Octavia. Neighborhood: Castro. Map: pg. 160.
Phone: (415) 431-1931.
Hours: Sun thru Thurs 7 p.m. to 1 a.m., Fri and Sat til 3 a.m.
Cover: $6.00 (An initial $12.00 membership fee is good for six months).

Since we abhor a mandatory clothes check and the 1808 requires it, we sent our friend the infamous Scott O'Hara to check out the situation. His report is as follows: The main drawback with the 1808 is price, making it the most expensive sex-spot between San Jose and Portland. The facilities, while decent and user-friendly, frankly are not worth it. Many years ago, the 1808 was a jack-off club, meaning that you could only suck and fuck if you were young, cute, and the owner invited you into the back room. But times and owners have changed; their new ad screams "SEX!" and indeed sucking is the order of the night. Fucking is still prohibited; on a busy night, when sightlines are obscured by bodies, perhaps one could get away with it. Therein, however, lies the problem: I have seen no nights that busy. The facilities are filled with innovative carpentry: ramps and balconies and closets and steps. Many benches are padded, and there are several comfortable (but cold) leather couches. I mention the temperature because they do have a mandatory clothes check. There are a couple of television monitors showing porn; a bar serving soft drinks and snacks; lots of mirrors everywhere you look (a couple of which, in the back-room, are dangerously shattered, with exposed sharp edges); humpy employees (who are often available at night's end, if you wanna stick around that long); and an amusing row of hairstylist sinks, intended for washing off your dick. Lighting varies; there are hot spots and dark corners.

The crowd: Well, when I arrived at 11 p.m. on a Friday night, there were a dozen men there. Eleven of them were quite attractive to me. Guess who followed me around all night, clinging to me like a leech until I finally asked him, "Don't I hear your mother calling?" The crowd had started thinning out by that time, but at about 12:30, there was an influx: the population swelled to around twenty. I played with several, including one who really knew how to get my engine racing. When I finally left at 1 a.m., I was tired but happy. The first Monday of the month, incidentally, is the "meating" of the S.F. Jacks, doors open 8 to 9 p.m. only. This is a dedicated group of wankers: there will often be sixty or seventy men packed into that relatively small space. Jack-off only, mandatory clothes check, and expect to get very sweaty and greasy. The lube of choice is Albolene.

The Black House

633 Castro bet. 19th and 20th Sts. (door on left). Neighborhood: Castro.
Map: pg. 160. Phone: (415) 863-6358.
Hours: Sun thru Thurs 8 p.m. til 2 a.m., Fri and Sat 9 p.m. til 6 a.m.
Cover: $8.00; $4.00 before 11 p.m.

A.k.a. Castro Party. This place, the most centrally located in the Castro, runs the gamut from wonderful to hideous. Lately it has been a little more than okay. The kitchen has the skimpiest of refreshments, often flat root beer and a stale bowl of chips. The scary refrigerator is known to some as the Jeffrey Dahmer Memorial fridge. Although the living room is equipped with a functional fireplace and video set-up, they don't use the fireplace enough, and every video we have ever seen there is yawnable. The split Victorian bathroom is usually well-stocked but has *no* locks for privacy. In Pansy's professional opinion, the bad artwork is just one more thing queens bump into. Art Alert: The piece in the front room over the "bed" is a bad palette scraping of the Velázquez's *Las Meniñas* (The Infanta and her dwarves), which Pansy recognized mid-blowjob. All three play rooms are equipped with nothing more than beds. The downstairs offers a large hallway that is so dark you cannot see your hand in front of your face. This is, of course, an advantage to the aesthetically challenged. The other "room" is only slightly more lit and appears to be a root cellar. There is a gloryhole wall but unfortunately folks only ever line up on one side. We advise you to take your trick under the stairs. The ever-rotating staff ranges from barely capable to laughable. Every time someone decent is hired, they inexplicably disappear. The only regular fixture seems to be Jim Coughenour.

Blow Buddies

933 Harrison bet. 5th and 6th Sts. Neighborhood: SOMA. Map: pg. 174.
Phone (415) 863-HEAD. Hours: Thurs 7:30 p.m. to 4 a.m. (no entry after 2:30
a.m.), Fri and Sat 9 p.m. to 6 a.m. (no entry after 4 a.m.), Sun 6 p.m. to 2 :30
a.m. (no entry after midnight). Cover: $7.00 to $9.00 (call hotline).

This place rocks so hard that it is difficult to describe it without gushing. When you arrive, you need to be a member
(which costs about $2.00 for six months). If you are not a
member, they generally like you to be "sponsored" the first
time you visit. Thus, if you are alone, tell them B&P sent
you. In the lobby, your courteous coat-check specialist awaits
you. You may check just about anything, and they take
awfully good care of it. The lobby also has lots of good literature regarding safe sex, AIDS, STDs, etc. There are two
restrooms. The front one has three stalls, while the rear bathroom has a trough urinal with mirrors strategically positioned
for optimum viewing and a nearby doorless stall with a gloryhole. The bathrooms are clean and are always well-stocked
with soap, paper towels, mouthwash (with hydrogen perox-
ide) and TP. The lounge area has a soda machine and a
clean, non-functional urinal filled with peanuts. They play
the hottest porn of the last three decades in the lounge and
maze areas. Pansy has noticed that the porn is all j/o and
blow, in keeping with the name and theme of this establishment.

Three major areas are always open: the booth room, the
bi-level room and the inner maze. All have their advantages.
Booths are highly coveted and hard to acquire. When someone exits one, act fast. We wish they were equipped with
ejector seats and timers to teach certain booth hogs lessons.
There are several different levels of gloryholes allowing one
to sit or stand while doing or being done. The outdoor space
is divided into two sections. One is for sex and is equipped
with booth and gloryholes and (as Pansy puts it) festive artwork. The other part is largely for socializing and smoking.
On some nights "Whiz World" is open. This room is for
Golden Shower enthusiasts. Sling Buddies, Golden Shower
Buddies (512-PISS), Leather Buddies (979-0242) and Hung
Buddies all meet different days and times. For information
send a SASE to Buddies/584 Castro St. #395/SF, CA 94114.

Eros

2051 Market at Church. Neighborhood: Castro. Map: pg. 160.
Events Line: (415) 864-3767. Hours: Mon thru Thurs 4 p.m. to midnight,
Fri 4 p.m. to 4 a.m., Sat 4 p.m. to 4 a.m., Sun 4 p.m. to 2 a.m.
Cover: $11.00 (plus a $7.00 membership fee good for six months).

This space offers a sauna, showers, a new European steam room, video lounges, slings, playrooms and a back-room maze. They also offer massage appointments and packages. To make an appointment or for more information, call (415) 255-4921 from 2 to 9 p.m. If you arrive before 7 p.m., admission is only $8.00. You can bring your own beer (in cans) and check it at the service counter. If you do not want to go south of Market to fulfill your urges, Eros is conveniently located near the Castro across from Safeway (irony intended?). Safe sex is promoted here—condoms, latex gloves and Wet lube are provided in each playroom. You are even quizzed at the door on what is and is not safe. The space is kind of like the baths without the water. Lockers are provided for clothing removal. Guests are strongly encouraged to remove it all, but allowed to keep either their underwear or a towel. There is a snack bar/social area downstairs; large playrooms upstairs are divided into labyrinths and cul-de-sacs. Large naugahyde mattresses and massage tables are scattered about, as are a barber's chair and a gynecological exam table. Why hasn't Eros become more popular? Perhaps it is not sleazy enough for some, and the suggested (but not mandatory) clothes check daunts others. Get there early (before midnight) for best results.

Mack

317 10th St. at Folsom. Neighborhood: SOMA. Map: pg. 174.
Phone: (415) 558-8300. Hours: 6 p.m. to 6 a.m., Fri and Sun open at 2 p.m.
Cover: $10.00 (requested donation).

We finally got around to visiting Mack again, and things are looking up. The first two times we tried to visit were "Sling" nights, for fist-fucking enthusiasts, so we passed. Opening the upstairs and back yard has made the place less claustrophobic, and the wattage has been increased so you can see who you are doing and being done by. They have mazes, gloryholes, videos, slings and a clothes check, which is not mandatory. Free refreshments consist of soda, hot dogs and weak coffee. The kitchen is the place to hang out and the only place to smoke. The bathrooms still offer no privacy.

The staff was friendly. The men ranged from scary trolls to cute white trash dudes, but they couldn't have been that bad, since we both played and had fun.

We had heard rumors of unsafe sex happening here. Despite the fact that Mack has its certificate of excellence from the "Coalition for Healthy Fascism (oops, Sex)," Pansy witnessed more unsafe sex here in one hour than she has ever witnessed at all the other "unsafe" venues decried by the coalition for the last nine years. This is a criticism of the "coalition," *not* of Mack. Though Mack isn't our cup of tea, it might be for you. Check it out. The clothes check is mandatory on Monday nights. Wednesday night is vacuum pumpers' night—bring your own pump. BYOB—cans only. Thursday is leather sex. The first, third and fifth Friday of each month, Mack is known as "Sling," for fist-fucking enthusiasts.

TEAROOMS

San Francisco is not known for its tearooms. When folks get picked up at the supermarket and can find a sex partner by sitting on their front steps, they rarely want to spend hours in a bathroom playing games. Some gay bars have cruisy bathrooms, but that doesn't mean any action occurs there. The cruisiest ones can be found at Badlands, Castro Station, Detour, Eagle, Hole in the Wall, Lonestar Saloon and My Place. We offer the following list of *rumored* leads for tearoom enthusiasts.

Duboce Park: nighttime only, usually the
    women's room—scary
Embarcadero #4, second level
Federal Building: Golden Gate Avenue, near General
    Services
Ferry Building: men's room at ferry waiting area in the
    evening
Ghirardelli Square, third floor men's room
Grand Hyatt, first basement level
Hyatt Regency: go across bridge from Embarcadero #4 and
    down one level
Japantown Bowl, second floor
Marina Green
Mother's Playground in Golden Gate Park
Playground at Chestnut and Fillmore
Rincon Center
San Francisco Shopping Center, mezzanine level
Sheraton Palace Hotel, basement
Sir Francis Drake Hotel, Sutter Street

THEATERS

Theaters usually offer porno on the big screen. Often there are added bonuses such as live strippers or appearances by porno stars. Some of these establishments also have video booths or small shops to boot. Though sex (in some form) happens at these places, they are not designed to encourage such activities, and the extent to which sex occurs often depends on the whim of the staff member on duty.

Campus Theater

220 Jones at Turk. Neighborhood: Tenderloin. Map: pg. 170.
Phone: (415) 673-3384 or 3383.
Hours: Sun thru Thurs 11 a.m. to midnight, Fri and Sat til 2 a.m.
Cover: $15.00 (with in/out privileges).

Thirteen live-nude shows daily, with additional Friday and Saturday late shows—call 673-3384 for times. Tuesday at 6 p.m. is the amateur show, which guarantees ten dollars to all participants and fifty dollars to the winner.

The ground floor consists of a lobby, two bathrooms with connecting gloryhole, and a theater where house strippers and porn stars frequently show their wares. Porn videos are shown between the strip acts. The sign outside the theater states that SF law prohibits audience members from touching the genitals or buttocks of performers. This issue seemed pretty moot as the performers straddled and then ground their body parts into the seated audience members. Audience regulars often have handfuls of dollar bills to stuff in the performers' socks since the only other place is prohibited by SF law. The strip squad, for the most part, consists of semi-attractive, sweaty, naked young men. They all make the rounds working everyone for tips, so if you don't like this kind of attention, it is advisable to stand near the back.

The basement is home to a tiny shower area, a family room-esque video area, a large non-functional bar, a maze and the arena. The arena has smaller well-lit strip shows, and customers often use it to grope each other in the dark between shows. Arena strip shows feature two naked guys who play with each other and then move through the audience by slowly stopping before each patron. Each of the two men circle the arena twice. Jerry, a devout SQR fan, informs us that the shower shows are a minimum of $20.00. A price is negotiated as the stripper crawls on the patron in the theater or arena areas. It is an opportunity for the rich and horny to spend more time with their favorite stripper, or strippers, in a more intimate atmosphere.

Circle J

369 Ellis bet. Taylor and Jones. Neighborhood: Tenderloin. Map: pg. 170.
Phone: (415) 474-6995. Hours: 10 a.m. to midnight. Cover: $8.00.

The films, changed on Sundays and Thursdays, are shown on three screens in the main auditorium. The main screen has three features; a second screen has j/o films, Grand Prix and Halcyon film exclusives; a third screen has classic film loops of the sixties and seventies. With all this running simultaneously, it gets a bit surreal. The theater is a rectangular room, and the seats are uncomfortable church pews. There is also a j/o room with monitor screens. Cruising is happening. Behind the main screen is an antechamber to the restroom with benches around the wall, an exposed throne and a large stainless steel sink with soap, water, and paper towels. The antechamber has two video screens. This place is exceptionally clean, and the films are exquisite.

Nob Hill Cinema

729 Bush at Powell. Neighborhood: Nob Hill. Map: pg. 170.
Phone: (415) 781-9468. Hours: 9 a.m. to 1:30 a.m.
Cover: free for arcade only; $20.00 for house ticket with in/out privileges.

The new owner is doing great things at the Nob Hill. He completely refurbished the arcade in the basement. Instead of antique quarter-token booths, he installed state-of-the-art booths that accept ones, fives, tens and twenties. Rumor has it they will soon accept ATM and major credit cards. When we were young, we trudged twenty miles in the snow to get blown in a booth for a penny. The new booths have one hundred twenty-one channels but no gloryholes (nor will there ever be). Buddy booths and group preview booths, which are big enough for four people and cost $12.00, are as close as you'll ever get. The staff doesn't seem to care if you are neighborly and share a booth, but you gotta keep the machine pumped full of cash. The addition of security cameras downstairs enables them to send someone to tell you to take a hike if you are not in a booth spending cash. There is also a new bathroom downstairs. The management wants the upstairs to be as state-of-the-art as the downstairs: they plan to totally refurbish the cinemas, eliminate the deck for smokers, and the merchandise has been moved upstairs. **99**

Blowjobs are allowed (even in the theater) but they will bust you so hard if you are fucking, with or without a condom. Under the new ownership, the dancers, unfortunately, aren't as hot as they once were—and there are fewer big name porno dudes. In his fifties, one of the regular dancers is one of the best; he has been doing it long enough to have his routine down. Sundays seem to be the busiest. The men are hot. Parking is difficult. If this place does go twenty-four seven, we predict it will be the hot new hangout.

The Tearoom Theater

145 Eddy bet. Mason and Taylor. Neighborhood: Tenderloin. Map: pg. 170.
Phone: (415) 885-9887.
Hours: Sun thru Thurs 9 a.m. to 2 a.m., Fri and Sat 24 hours. Cover: $7.50.

Monday thru Friday, 9 a.m. to 10 a.m., they offer an early-bird admission special of $5.00 and a bizarre system of in/out passes. Call the number listed to get the details. A message will also give you the strippers' "names" and the times of shows: Monday thru Thursday at 12, 2, 5:30 and 7:30 p.m., Fri at 12, 2, 5:30, 7:30, 9 and 11 p.m., Sat at 1, 4, 5:30, 7:30, 9 and 11 p.m., and Sun at 1, 4, 5:30, and 7:30 p.m. The amateur performances can be quite frightening. The whole experience was very seedy. Pansy recognized many hateful people, including a guy Pansy refers to as Little Hitler, who was dressed in a polyester leisure suit. There are free lockers, live jack-off shows and a number of porn films playing simultaneously on the main screen and in the back lounge. Films change on Monday and Friday.

VIDEO ARCADES

Video arcades generally show porn films in individual booths for a quarter (or the equivalent token) for approximately one minute's time. Often they are popular with gay men because of the peepholes or gloryholes that are sometimes drilled by an ambitious Lurky Turkey. You can generally tell which cater to gay men and which to straight by the percentage of gay versus straight porn films in the arcade. Anything approaching fifty percent means that many of the customers are gay.

When visiting for the first time, pay attention to staff and patrons to get an idea of what kind of activity is allowed, which is usually up to the whim of the person on duty. Generally, the staff doesn't mind if guys jump in booths together or do each other through gloryholes, as long as quarters or tokens are being dropped. Isn't capitalism beautiful? Also, watch for "buddy booths": a phenomenon that occurs when two separate booths are connected by a smoked window. When you drop your quarter in the slot, the window turns "on." If your neighbor drops his quarter as well, then the "fog" disappears, and you can see each other clearly. Buddy booths are great for "previewing" someone. If you change your mind, simply hit the "off" button, or wait for your time to expire on the video. Unfortunately, the same thing can happen to you—it is a rather cold and impersonal gimmick but quite effective and interesting.

City Entertainment

960 Folsom bet. 5th and 6th Sts. Neighborhood: SOMA. Map: pg. 174.
Phone: (415) 543-2124.
Hours: Sun thru Thurs 8 a.m. to 3 a.m., Fri and Sat open 24 hours.

This is the best video booth spot. There are twelve booths and two viewing booths for those rich queens who want to pay $5.00 to preview porno tapes. Booths 1 & 2 and 3 & 4 are buddy booths. The best booths are 11, 6 and 5. Generally bustling, this place is great after work and in the late evening. If you have enough money, you can spend hours here. The boys are getting hotter and hotter. A word to the wise: Put your finger through and all around a glory-hole before putting your dick through it—trust us.

The staff here has never given the customers a hard time of any sort. It costs $2.00 to enter the arcade, but get more tokens. Bring smaller bills because they don't break twenties, and the machine in the back only takes ones and fives. Also there is no water fountain, so save a dollar in quarters for the soda machine. The bathroom at this establishment is usually unclean, and the door does not lock.

Folsom Gulch

947 Folsom bet. 5th and 6th Sts. Neighborhood: SOMA. Map: pg. 174.
Phone: (415) 495-6402. Hours: 10 a.m. to 3 a.m., Fri and Sat open 24 hours.

Features twelve standard video booths and two preview booths, including buddy booths and oddly shaped gloryholes. Recent reconstruction allows you to circle all twelve booths, and there is a new bathroom that affords no privacy but does allow one to take a whiz and wash his hands. This place attracts a slightly older and rougher crowd than City Entertainment across the street. A friend informed me that before he got sober, he once came here high. He climbed on top of his booth and crawled around watching folks have sex for hours. He thought he was real swift until he walked out and realized he was covered from head to toe in dust bunnies and had the chicken-wire pattern imprinted on his pants from the knee down.

Frenchy's

1020 Geary bet. Polk and Van Ness. Neighborhood: Polk. Map: pg. 168.
Phone: (415) 776-5940. Hours: 24 hours, 7 days a week.

You have to buy three dollars' worth of tokens to enter the arcade, which is quite large—at least two dozen booths—and not very clean or too well-lit. There is, however, a huge assortment of dildos and other sex-toy paraphernalia. The clientele ranges in age, race and class status. Extremely hit-or-miss, this place is usually fairly empty, but occasionally you will discover a yummy character. They do have a security guard that sometimes makes rounds in the evening, and they are quite intent on the policy that if you are occupying a booth you must drop tokens.

Recently, a tragedy occurred here that made the papers: apparently someone stuck his dick through a gloryhole and the dude on the other side poured some sort of acid on it. The perpetrator got away. The victim of this bizarre crime had nothing to soothe his searing peter so he bought a soda and used that. By the way, there is no bathroom, which is a total bummer.

The Locker Room

1038 Polk at Geary. Neighborhood: Polk. Map: pg. 168.
Phone: (415) 775-9076. Hours: 24 hours, 7 days a week.

Instead of battling the hustlers who want you to give them a blowjob for five dollars, why not get one for free where the guy won't be tweaking? The Locker Room is new and clean, with spacious booths and huge television screens. The bathroom, however, is almost never functional. The staff is hypervigilant regarding the continuous use of tokens, not the sexual activity inside. Although the staff is generally less than pleasant, we would be too if we had to work on lower Polk.

Mission News

2086 Mission between 16th and 17th Sts. Neighborhood: Mission. Map: pg. 176.
Phone: (415) 626-0309. Hours: 24 hours, 7 days a week.

This place used to be so much fun. Since the remodeling job, however, there are few gloryholes and peepholes and no circle to walk around. There are two sides. On the left, four of the twelve token booths are dedicated to two sets of buddy booths. The right side has about ten five-dollar preview booths. Video cameras are being used to watch for trouble and bark at folks for excessive loitering, not to bust guys for sex. The disgusting bathroom has no sink and rarely has any toilet paper.

You work out . . .
right?

Gyms

If you are queer and enjoy playing sports with other queers, San Francisco is the place for you. Some information and listings can be found in the *Bay Area Reporter (B.A.R.)*, *Bay Times*, or *Frontiers*. A gay and lesbian group is organized around every sport imaginable. Some even make their way to the Queer Olympics (oops, Gay Games).

There are a number of gyms in SF. The queerest ones we know are listed below. To find out more 'bout each, call the phone number.

Central YMCA

220 Golden Gate Ave. Neighborhood: Tenderloin. Map: pg. 170. Phone: (415) 885-0460.

Good for beginners, the poor and women. Men in showers with full hard-ons, touch pee-pee in the steam room and sauna, and sex by the punching bag in the eighth-floor bathroom or on the roof. People cruise all over.

City Athletic

2500 Market. Neighborhood: Castro. Map: pg. 160. Phone: (415) 552-6680.

Used to be the dumping ground for old clones. Lately, things have been looking up with a modicum of hot boys and the occasional porno star. A.k.a. Sissy Athletic, Shitty Athletic.

Gold's Gym

333 Valencia bet. 14th and 15th Sts. Neighborhood: Mission. Map: pg. 176. Phone: (415) 626-8865.

For folks truly into the body-building experience. A source informs us that the showers are massively cruisy and the gay boys act as if the straight boys aren't there.

Gorilla Sports

501 2nd St. Square. Neighborhood: SOMA. Map: pg. 174. Phone: (415) 777-4653.

For guppys (gay urban professionals) looking for husbands.

Market Street Gym

2301 Market. Neighborhood: Castro. Map: pg. 160. Phone: (415) 626-4488.

The only queer co-ed gym we know. Very social, cruisy and spotlessly clean. The men's jacuzzi is known as the "jizz-cuzzi" or "the protein pool."

Muscle Systems

2275 Market. Neighborhood: Castro. Map: pg. 160. Phone: (415) 863-4700.

A.k.a. Muscle Sisters and Muscle Sissies. For the older guys. Has a cruisy sauna.

Muscle Systems

364 Hayes. Neighborhood: Hayes Valley. Map: pg. 165. Phone: (415) 863-4701.

Has a more beautiful and youthful crowd. A little groping happens in the jacuzzi. The sauna is known for eye contact, obvious erections, and surreptitious fondling of one's own genitals. With the help of strategically located mirrors, the sauna and jacuzzi have views of both the locker room and showers. The gym itself is not very cruisy—a place to get dates but not sex.

Women's Training Center

2164 Market bet. Sanchez and Church. Neighborhood: Duboce Triangle. Map: pg. 160. Phone: (415) 864-6835.

See Lesbians & Dykes, Queer Culture (page 120) for information.

World Gym

260 Deharo. Neighborhood: Potrero Hill. Map: pg. 157. Phone: (415) 703-9650.

The graduate school of gyms, where the big and beautiful boys go—no skinnies or fatties. Folks are serious about working out, and cruising is at a minimum.

Lesbian with a
Hard-On

Lesbians & Dykes

In San Francisco there are more kinds of lesbians than you can shake a stick at. Some identify as fag boys, some as leather-dykes, some as super lipstick lezzies, and the list goes on and on. No matter how you identify, if you are a woman who gets it on with other women, we hope that there is something of interest to you in this chapter.

BARS, CLUBS AND HANGOUTS

Avalon

Phone: (415) 487-6305. Cover $7.00.

Avalon is a women's night club that happens the last Saturday of each month. Call to find out present location.

Club Ecstasy

960 Harrison bet. 5th and 6th Sts. Neighborhood: SOMA. Map: pg. 174.
Phone: (415) 985-5252

Flier reads, "The hottest concept in lesbian erotic environments." Hmmmm. $49.00 for a one-year membership or $20.00 for a one-night membership. Checks, ATM and credit cards accepted. Lesbians (not dykes, they're too poor to afford it and have bad credit anyway) actually have sex here on occasion. More of a lipstick lesbo crowd than anything, although leather dykes wander in here from time to time looking for empty wall space to chain up some unsuspecting neophyte (kidding, just kidding). It runs monthly; might be worth the $20.00 to check it out at least once.

Coco Club

139 8th St. at Minna. Neighborhood: SOMA. Map: pg. 174.
Phone: (415) 626-2337.

This bar seems to have popped up out of nowhere. No one can confirm if it is actually a seven-night-a-week dyke spot, but it seems to be open more often than one would expect. Located in a basement, the space is small but mighty fun. Betty had the honor of performing at Sister Spit, a spoken-word series for dykes only—they made a rare exception for her. The series takes place on Sunday nights about once a month. Coco Club frequently hosts rockin' dyke bands. Keep your eyes and ears open, and check out this spot.

GirlSpot

278 11th St. at Folsom (VSF). Neighborhood: SOMA. Map: pg. 174.
Phone: (415) 337-4962. Hours: 8 p.m. to 2 a.m.
Cover: $6.00 after 10 p.m., less before 10 p.m. M/F: 7/93.

Practically an institution as San Francisco's longest running and most popular dance club for women, GirlSpot (or G-Spot,

"If you can't find it, you can't come") attracts a real cross section of women. Most are of the suburban variety, but city dykes are represented as well. The club's newest home, the recently refurbished VSF, lends itself nicely to cruising. The roof patio is spacious, and the dance floor is generally packed with people getting down to the modern club mixes. Other features include go-go dancers, contests and promotions. Every dyke comes here at least once because the G-Spot has so much to offer. You can see just about anyone here at any-time. For those super fancy dykes, valet parking is available. Since this is the third or fourth space G-Spot has inhabited in about five years, it is wise to call the above number to insure that the location is the same.

Hollywood Billiards

61 Golden Gate Ave. at Market. Neighborhood: Civic Centre. Map: pg. 157.
Phone: (415) 252-9643. Hours: 11 a.m. to 2 a.m. M/F: 20/80.

This pool hall hosts a fabulous Wednesday night chickfest. Women play pool for free all night. Free pool equals tons of poor dykes, with a variety of lezzies from leather to quasi-Birkenstock clad. There is a minimal het factor; as we all know, however, the minimum can be annoying. WARNING: *Do not go any other night. Rrr. Rrr.* This place also has a bar and snacky food.

Litter Box

683 Clementina at 8th St. (Cat's Alley Bar & Grill). Neighborhood: SOMA.
Map: pg. 174. Phone: DNA. Hours: Friday nights only, 10 p.m. to 3 a.m.
Cover: $5.00. M/F: 50/50.

You can expect just about anything once you step inside this place, which has become so popular that, at times, there is a line to get in. No guaranteeing what gender you'll go home with at the end of the evening. Junkyard and Javier are the DJs, and anything that involves Junkyard is great fun for dykes of the nineties. She is one girl on the go. They play everything from Dolly Parton to Metallica to Donna Summer. Occasionally, live performances take place in the front room.

MT Productions

584 Castro St., Suite #206 / San Francisco, CA 94114. Phone: (415) 337-4962.

This production company hosts huge parties and successful clubs for women throughout the year. MT Productions is **111** responsible for GirlSpot (see above) and Club Skirts. MT also hosts events out of town like the Dinah Shore Weekend in Palm Springs. For detailed information, call the events line listed above and get on their mailing list.

Muffdive

527 Valencia at 16th St. (Casanova Bar). Neighborhood: Mission. Map: pg. 176. Phone: DNA. Hours: Sun nights only, 10 p.m. to 2 a.m. Cover: $3.00. M/F: 5/95.

A long-running (two-and-a-half years is long by San Francisco dyke standards) Sunday night club, this is at times *the* place for cool dykes—note: dykes, not lesbians. If you don't know the difference, this is probably not your kinda space. The recent incarnation on Valencia Street lets in boys (eiwww). While one or two fags can definitely perk up any club, more than that at the 'dive completely fucks it up. Small, usually packed, it's a mix between post-punk shaved-head grrrls and raucous Gap-clad bar dykes. If you are not the type who enjoys G-Spot's attitude and cheap knockoff imitation designer fragrances, then Muffdive is probably more your speed. Recommended for dykes that like to socialize in a riot grrrl sort of space.

Pussycat Hotline

(415) 561-9771

This is the information number for the occasional wild dyke clubs, Faster Pussycat and Snatch ("Where the rude queers roam"). Call the number listed for more information.

Red

Blondie's Bar No Grill, 540 Valencia at 16th St. Neighborhood: Mission. Map: pg. 176. Phone: (415) 864-2419.

Tuesday nights are dyke nights with fun, hip-hop music. Loads of cultural diversity, which rocks in this segregated town. Lots of gorgeous dark-haired women. The small space is packed. They'll kick your ass if you touch that hanging light over the dance floor.

Red Dora's Bearded Lady Café and Gallery

485 14th St. at Guerrero. Neighborhood: Mission. Map: pg. 176.
Phone: (415) 626-2805.

This café and art gallery, owned, operated and patronized by dykes, is a great spot to just hang out during the day if you are a dyke. They have a limited vegetarian menu, are smoke- and alcohol-free, and wheelchair accessible. On occasion, they host an evening of spoken-word performance curated by Kris Kovick, the famous lezzie cartoonist. The coolest dyke writers, poets, filmmakers, columnists, comedians, and other cultural workers show up to do their thing. Betty has performed here on several occasions. The house is always packed, and the crowd is always appreciative. The cover is generally $5.00. Arrive early as Red Dora's is popular and space is limited.

Urban Womyn's Land

3690 18th St. near Dolores. Neighborhood: Mission. Map: pg. 176.
Phone: (415) 267-2161.
Hours: Fri 5 to 11 p.m., Sat noon to 7 p.m., and Sun noon to 10 p.m.
Cover: donation requested. M/F: 0/100.

A.k.a. Whiptail Lizard Lounge. This is a weekend-only, women-only happening, a wildly diverse group of women looking for wimmin-only space in the middle of white-gay-male hell. A leather-friendly place, they welcome all dykes. Dudes are cool if under the age of ten. The Whiptail ranges from being chatty to sleepy: a nice place to enjoy a sunny day and a book; check out their lending library. Sodas and bagels are for sale. This is an alcohol-, drug- and smoke-free environment.

Wild Side West

424 Cortland at Wool. Neighborhood: Bernal Heights. Map: pg. 157.
Phone: (415) 647-3099. Hours: 1 p.m. to 2 a.m. M/F: 20/80.

Alright, here's the deal: When we were first doing research for the book, we had never heard of this spot. We visited, we hung out, we loved it, and we gave it a rave review. Here, in part, is what we wrote: "This super cool dyke bar celebrated its thirtieth anniversary in November 1991. The backyard is used for live music, poetry readings, etc. Oldest women's bar in the city. Interior includes an altar to podiatry, Mona Lisa peering out of a golden toilet seat, cut-out snowflakes on the walls, and real live barber chairs (bikini wax anyone?). Pool table is busy, so get in line on chalkboard. Very friendly atmosphere—perfect for Chatty Cathys like us. Pretty mixed crowd: straight people from the neighborhood as well as a few queers and the right-on dykes. Pansy says, 'What my home would be like if I lived alone, without the pinball machines.' People are having food delivered, and there is a football game on the television. Walls are a museum of lesbian eclecticism and herstory. Very homey and friendly. Jukebox selections include 'Take a Walk on the Wild Side,' 'Paradise by the Dashboard Light' and 'Fever.' Betty performed 'Fever' and people were into it. One pool table, two pinball machines and one computer game."

Well, Pansy returned aglow to show them our handiwork. The owners (two women who we have been told are partners of over thirty years) were aghast. They informed us that Wild Side West was not a lesbian bar but a neighborhood bar. Excuse us. The gay papers also recently reported that a lesbian couple was evicted for public displays of affection. The Lesbian Avengers responded with a kiss-in. We asked an Avenger we know how the owners responded to said action. She said they didn't care because they were selling lots of drinks. So here is our new review: This is a neighborhood bar in Bernal Heights (an area populated by lesbian homeowners). When you come through the door, do not be dismayed by a half-dozen middle-aged women with salt-and-pepper brush cuts smoking cigars and playing cards—they are just neighbors. The interior of the bar is a delight and says much about the history of the neighborhood. The two female owners (apparently good friends and roommates) opened this establishment over thirty years ago. If you are a neighbor, you might like it.

L O D G I N G

Listed from least expensive to most expensive.

Nancy's Bed

Neighborhood: Twin Peaks. Map: pg. 156. Phone: (415) 239-5692.
Rates: $20.00 per person per night.

This private lesbian home for women travelers is only five minutes by car to the Castro and close to public transit (both MUNI and BART). A refundable deposit is required, and tourist information for lesbians is available. Smoking is allowed on the deck only.

Carl Street Unicorn House

156 Carl. Neighborhood: The Haight. Map: pg. 164. Phone: (415) 753-5194.
Rates: $40.00 - 50.00. E-mail: unicorn@desart.com.

This bed and breakfast is also the home of the proprietor, Miriam Weber. It was built in 1895 and has only two bed-rooms for guests, who must share one bathroom. Located near Golden Gate Park and the Haight-Ashbury District, Unicorn House is also close to Tassajara Bakery (yum). A television and a piano are available in the living room; rates include an extended continental breakfast. This is a non-smoking house.

Bock's Bed and Breakfast

1448 Willard. Neighborhood: The Haight. Map: pg. 164. Phone: (415) 664-6842.
Rates: $40.00 - 75.00.

Near Golden Gate Park and UC Medical Center, this B&B is a drive or bus ride to the Castro. There is a two-night minimum with a required deposit, and weekly rates are available. Bock's offers three units, each with phones, coffee/tea service and access to a refrigerator. Continental breakfast is served in the dining room. Smoking is prohibited.

House O' Chicks

2162 15th St. near Noe. Neighborhood: Castro. Map: pg. 160.
Phone: (415) 861-9849. Rates: $50.00 - 75.00.

This Victorian offers you a lesbian household in the Castro. Amenities include the use of the kitchen, office, PC and laser printer, and fax machine. Higher rates during holidays and Gay Pride.

QUEER CULTURE

Black & Blue Tattoo

483 14th St. at Guerrero. Neighborhood: Mission. Map: pg. 176.
Phone: (415) 626-0770. Hours: 12 to 9 p.m. everyday.

This is a dyke-owned and -operated tattoo parlor. If you are visiting San Francisco and get that urge to be marked for life, then this is the place to go. The staff is ultra-cool and will make this experience much easier for a newcomer. You don't have to be a lezzie either. These chiquitas would love to take thousands of high speed needles to boy flesh as well.

Brick Hut Café

2512 San Pablo at Dwight Way, Berkeley, CA. Map: pg. 159.
Phone: (510) 486-1124.
Hours: 8 a.m. to 3 p.m. for breakfast and lunch;
5 to 10 p.m. on Wed, Thurs, Fri, Sat for dinner.

From our reviewer's perspective, the entire staff was peopled with dykes. We were also informed that they are total babes and not really the usual East Bay types (big granola heads). There is usually an extremely long wait for this very popular restaurant as it is *the* lesbian spot to eat in the East Bay. The food is very good and moderately priced, and the spacious new location is a vast improvement over the last one. Despite everything else, the main attraction is the pervasive lesbian atmosphere.

Castlebar

141 8th St. at Minna. Neighborhood: SOMA. Map: pg. 174.
Phone: (415) 552-2100.

This house is dyke-owned and host to het sessions by day, as well as various S/M play parties throughout the month, most notably Sarah Lashes' monthly soirees. Call for details. Terrific lesbian S/M action but be sure to ask for dyke night. Glory is solely defined by the patrons of this establishment (i.e. avoid heterosexual parties at all costs, trust us). Our friend Peg attended one and reported witnessing drooling pig men who did not know squat about S/M. When it's time to leave, wait inside and call for your cab. The neighborhood is not pretty and does not appreciate full fetish drag.

Eros

2051 Market at Church. Neighborhood: Castro. Map: pg. 160.
Events line: (415) 864-3767. Office line: (415) 255-4921.

This sex club has hosted numerous women-only nights, such as Sluts for Sensation. Give the office a call to see if and when more events for women will be happening.

Gaia Books Music & Café

Shattuck at Rose, Berkeley, CA. Map: pg. 159. Phone: (510) 548-4172.

This East Bay women's bookstore carries goddess-oriented ritual supplies, as well as women's biography, spirituality, psychology and health books. They also sell and rent videos and hold author events. They stress that though this is a woman's bookstore, men are welcome.

Good Vibrations

1210 Valencia at 23rd St. Neighborhood: Mission. Map: pg. 176.
Phone: (415) 974-8980. Hours: 11 a.m. to 7 p.m. every day.

A really cool shop for sex supplies. They carry hundreds of different vibrators, dildos, harnesses, books, magazines and other paraphernalia. This is a modern queer sex superstore. Excellent for the timid, closeted or novice wannabe sex guru. Browsing is encouraged. The store is clean, and the mostly female staff is friendly. S/M friendly. Fun if you like your sex clean and well-lit. Has been discovered by the breeder set, but we all know that our straight sisters need vibrators, too.

Lesbian Avengers

Phone: (415) 267-6195.

Betty recently found herself in the Marina—the straight yuppy neighborhood that will hopefully collapse in the next quake. She was celebrating a birthday with a friend when she spotted a dyke co-worker. She raced outside to say hi and was greeted by whoops and cheers from about thirty lesbians. It was the Lesbian Avengers. They had decided to terrorize the straightest neighborhood in the city as it was National Coming Out Day. These lesbian, bisexual and transgendered women concoct and execute the smartest, wittiest and politically wisest actions for Lesbian survival and visibility. Every Monday, 7 to 9 p.m. at 1360 Mission, Room 200, "Queer Central."

Luna Sea

2940 16th St. at Mission, Rm. 216 C. Neighborhood: Mission. Map: pg. 176. Phone: (415) 863-2989.

This performance space showcases all kinds of dyke performances and art. The patrons are similar to Red Dora's set of grrrls, but the space is larger and isn't a café. If you're in town, call to find out what's being featured. There is an extraordinarily high concentration of fabulous queer, grunge, butch, femme, hot dykes and a few cool fags. Luna Sea hosted the very popular BUILT, readings and performances by and about butch dykes. They also plan on hosting Death On Heels II, about femme-identity. Check this spot out.

Lyon-Martin Women's Health Services

1748 Market, Suite 201. Neighborhood: Hayes Valley. Map: pg. 165. Phone: (415) 565-7667.

LMWHS, a fifteen-year-old nonprofit organization, provides the following services: primary medical care for women; medical care, case management and nutrition counseling to HIV-positive women; HIV prevention services for women; substance abuse prevention services for women; parenting services, youth services and smoking cessation services for the lesbian, gay, bisexual and transgender community. LMWHS is the only autonomous community clinic in the U.S. with a primary emphasis on lesbian and bisexual women's health care. They take sliding-scale payments, and the staff is very friendly and professional.

Mama Bear's

6536 Telegraph at Ashby, Oakland, CA. Map: pg. 159. Phone: (510) 428-9684.

Well-known as a spacious and comfy coffeehouse for socializing, this women's bookstore is virtually an institution. Besides books, they carry women's jewelry, crafts, music, and much more. No lesbian trip to the East Bay would be complete without visiting this historic spot. Open every day.

Osento Baths

955 Valencia bet. 20th and 21st Sts. Neighborhood: Mission. Map: pg. 176.
Phone: (415) 282-6333. Hours: 1 p.m. to 1 a.m. (doors close at midnight).
Rates: $7.00 to $10.00 (sliding scale).

This is a bathhouse—not a sex club. In fact, sex is expressly forbidden by the house rules, but don't let that stop you from going. Osento has a distinctively New Age feel—from piped-in music to the complimentary spring water with lemons. With two saunas, a giant hot tub, cold plunge (outside), and steam huts, Osento is an excellent place to unwind and cleanse yourself. Let's not forget—it's full of naked women. (We do happen to know some "wild grrrls" who have done the nasty here.) Private masseuse available for extra fee; call for rate/appointments. There is a one dollar charge for towel use. Super-packed on weekend nights, Osento is not a bar or a softball diamond, but a totally diverse set of women that would never meet otherwise.

Pervert Scouts

Phone: (415) 285-7985.

They rock and rule. Pervert Scouts is headed by the infamous Kiki S. Carr who works at Damron by day, is a punk/nerd, and some would say, the heir apparent to the Goddess Matriarch S/M throne. She founded and facilitates this dis-cussion/workshop/cruise spot/informal gathering that meets one Saturday a month at Luna Sea (see page 118). They fea-ture monthly speakers, demos, and chit chat about how to get more bang for your buck. Loads of fun, super informal. Newcomers are always welcome.

QSM

P.O. Box 880154/San Francisco, CA 94188.
Phone: (415) 550-7776 or (800) 537-5815. Fax: (415) 550-7117.

An informational organization offering weekly workshops and mini book-and-catalog store by appointment only. Workshops include breath games, mastering the single-tail, and sundry aspects of sadomasochism—classes on the basics that are a must for any novice. They have an extensive mail-ing list. Get on it.

Stormy Leather

1158 Howard at 7th St. Neighborhood: SOMA. Map: pg. 174.
Phone: (415) 626-1672.

Stormy Leather, the biggest fetish-outfit store for women in town, carries anything you want from floggers and cats to clamps and clips. Much of the stuff is made on the premises, and latex clothing is a specialty. The prices are a bit steep unless you volunteer to strip naked and be chained to a wall for an hour. Kidding, just kidding. The breeder set is a major funder; those straight guys have money to burn. Too bad Jenne Blade does not work here anymore; she was our favorite employee. The gorgeous boots on display range widely in size. Stormy Leather is the place to go for fetish wear and accompanying cultural taboos. Say hi to Shadow.

West Berkeley Women's Books

2514 San Pablo at Dwight, Berkeley, CA. Map: pg. 159. Phone: (510) 204-9399.

This woman-owned and -operated bookstore in West Berkeley is another one to check out on your East Bay expedition. Keep in mind that they are closed Mondays and Tuesdays.

Women's Action Coalition (WAC)

1360 Mission at 10th St., Suite 200. Neighborhood: Mission. Map: pg. 176.
Phone: (415) 282-8900.

Meetings are the first and third Tuesday of each month at 7:30 p.m.

Women's Training Center

2164 Market bet. Sanchez and Church. Neighborhood: Duboce Triangle.
Map: pg. 160. Phone: (415) 864-6835.
Hours: Mon thru Fri 6 a.m. to 10 p.m., Sat 8 a.m. to 8 p.m., Sun 10 a.m. to 5 p.m.

Services include Cybex-Eagle fitness systems, free weights, aerobic conditioning, treadmills, stairmasters, versaclimber, lifecycles, recumbent bicycles, powerlifting, bodybuilding, sauna, massage, and individualized instruction. This women-only gym is a five minute walk from the Castro. The clientele includes lots of hot dykes, but they are there to work out, not to cruise. The staff is very friendly and helpful. The machines are in demand during the 5 - 7 p.m. rush hour, but you rarely have to wait long, and it is almost never crowded at other times. Call for information on membership rates.

P.C. Gal

Having the Time of Her Life

I'll be your bed
if you'll be my breakfast!

Lodging

While in San Francisco, gay and lesbian tourists most frequently stay in the following places. Other options for women are listed in Lesbians & Dykes, Lodging (page 115). We have tried to include a range from dirt cheap to the more upscale. They are listed in that order.

American Youth Hostels

Golden Gate Council, 425 Divisadero, Suite 307. Neighborhood: Hayes Valley. Map: pg. 165.

These folks offer hostel memberships; international student I.D. cards; Eurail passes issued the same day; student and charter flights; lowest prices on M.E.I. travel packs in SF; a wide selection of travel books, maps, and biking and hiking guides; and free use of the travel library. The nightly rate is usually $3.00 more for non-members. Mattress, pillow and blankets are provided, and linens can be rented. Remember that guests contribute to hostel upkeep by doing a brief chore each morning. Hostels are smoke-, alcohol- and drug-free; they usually have a curfew as well. There are two hostels within San Francisco:

San Francisco International

Bldg. 240, Fort Mason. Neighborhood: Marina. Map: pg. 165.
Phone: (415) 771-7277. Rates: $13.00 per night.

This hostel has 160 beds and overlooks the Golden Gate Bridge.

San Francisco Downtown

312 Mason. Neighborhood: Union Square. Map: pg. 171. Phone: (415) 788-5604. Rates: $15.00 a night for members and $18.00 for non-members.

This location has 175 beds. Most rooms accommodate two people and have a private bath. There is no curfew—guests have twenty-four-hour access—and it is located downtown, near Union Square, theaters, shopping and museums.

Pension

1668 Market at Gough. Neighborhood: Civic Centre. Map: pg. 157.
Phone: (415) 864-1271. Rates: $35.00 - 55.00.

This European-style hotel offers an extensive continental breakfast; restaurant and bar; laundry/dry cleaning, maid and concierge service; stocked refrigerators, direct-dial telephones and hair dryers in each room. This place is centrally located—about a fifteen minute walk to the Castro and close to the Mission and SOMA. To get public transportation, all you have to do is walk out the front door.

The Leland Hotel

1315 Polk at Bush. Neighborhood: Polk. Map: pg. 168.
Phone: (415) 441-5141 or (800) 258-4458. Rates: $40.00 - 58.00.

If you want to stay in the Polk Street area, this is the queer choice, with color televisions and phones in each room.

Travelodge

1707 Market at Valencia. Neighborhood: Castro. Map: pg. 160.
Phone: (415) 621-6775 or (800) 255-3050.
Rates: $49.00 and up.

This is not necessarily a "queer" establishment, but several readers have written to tell us that the staff very often is. Centrally located near SOMA, the Mission and the Castro.

24 Henry

24 Henry bet. Sanchez and Noe. Neighborhood: Duboce Triangle. Map: pg. 160.
Phone: (415) 864-5686 or (800) 900-5686. Rates: $55.00 - 90.00.

This B&B in Duboce Triangle is a restored one-hundred-twenty-two-year-old Victorian. The entire house is non-smoking.

Beck's Motor Lodge

2222 Market bet. Sanchez and Noe. Neighborhood: Duboce Triangle. Map: pg. 160.
Phone: (415) 621-8212 or (800) 227-4360. Rates: $59.00 - 95.00.

Although not necessarily queer-owned or -operated, this place is in the middle of the Castro. Services include free in-room coffee, refrigerators, color television, free HBO, direct-dial phones, private baths, and parking.

Le Grenier

347 Noe at Market. Neighborhood: Castro. Map: pg. 160. Phone: (415) 864-4748. Rates: $60.00 - 75.00.

This B&B, located in the heart of the Castro, offers light cooking facilities, telephone, television, and a continental breakfast.

The Willows

710 14th St. Neighborhood: Upper Market. Map: pg. 160. Phone: (415) 431-4770. Rates: $70.00 - 125.00.

Housed in a 1904 Edwardian, The Willows derives its name from the hand-crafted bentwood willow furnishings that grace each room. The Willows is a shared-bath inn with a wash basin in each of their eleven rooms and eight separate bath facilities. Kimono bathrobes are provided. Each morning, breakfast and a newspaper are delivered to your room. When you return at night, these friendly folks have turned on your light, turned down your bed and poured you a glass of port.

Black Stallion Inn

635 Castro bet. 19th and 20th Sts. Neighborhood: Castro. Map: pg. 160. Phone: (415) 863-0131. Rates: $80.00 - 110.00.

San Francisco's only leather-Levi's-western bed and breakfast is located right in the Castro. A microwave, refrigerator and fireplace occupy the common room. The Black Stallion also has a large sunny deck. Complimentary breakfast is served from 9 a.m. to 11 a.m. daily.

Inn on Castro

321 Castro bet. Market and 16th St. Neighborhood: Castro. Map: pg. 160. Phone: (415) 861-0321. Rates: $75.00 -135.00.

Services include living room with fireplace, complimentary brandy, complimentary full breakfast, private baths (for most rooms), and color televisions (on request).

The Inn San Francisco

943 South Van Ness. Neighborhood: Mission. Map: pg. 176. Phone: (415) 641-0188 or (800) 359-0913. Rates: $75.00 - 195.00.

Originally built on Mansion Row in the early 1870's, this historic twenty-seven-room Italianate Victorian has been converted into a bed and breakfast with a flower garden, a roof-top sun deck, and a gazebo, which houses the hot tub. The interior is filled with ornate woodwork, oriental carpets, marble fireplaces, beveled and stained glass, and antique furnishings. Rates include breakfast; use of hot tub, sun deck and gardens; and complimentary tea and coffee. Each room comes with a clock radio, telephone, small refrigerator and a color television.

The Chateau Tivoli

The Jackson-Kreling House, 1057 Steiner. Neighborhood: Pacific Heights. Map: pg. 165. Phone: (415) 776-5462 or (800) 228-1647. Rates: $80.00 - 300.00.

Formerly the Langtry, this self-dubbed "opulent bed and breakfast" is a landmark mansion located on Alamo Square. The building is completely non-smoking and has major historic and architectural significance. The entire place is filled with antiques and art from the Vanderbilt, DeGaulle, Richelieu, Getty and Stanford collections. They provide a continental-plus breakfast.

The Albion House Inn

135 Gough bet. Oak and Page. Neighborhood: Hayes Valley. Map: pg. 165. Phone: (415) 621-0896 or (800) 6ALBION. Rates: $85.00 - 195.00.

This B&B in Hayes Valley has a central living room with a fireplace for the guests to enjoy. All rooms have private baths, direct-dial phones and color televisions.

The Villa

379 Collingwood bet. 20th and 21st Sts. Neighborhood: Castro. Map: pg. 160. Phone: (415) 282-1367 or (800) 358-0123. Rates: $110.00 - 130.00.

Housed in the Castro, these executive suites and rooms are decorated in a modern/deco style. The lounge area contains a piano and fireplace, and offers views of the San Francisco skyline. A large deck with barbecue facilities and an expansive patio surrounding a heated swimming pool are also at your disposal. There is also a studio apartment available by day, week or month.

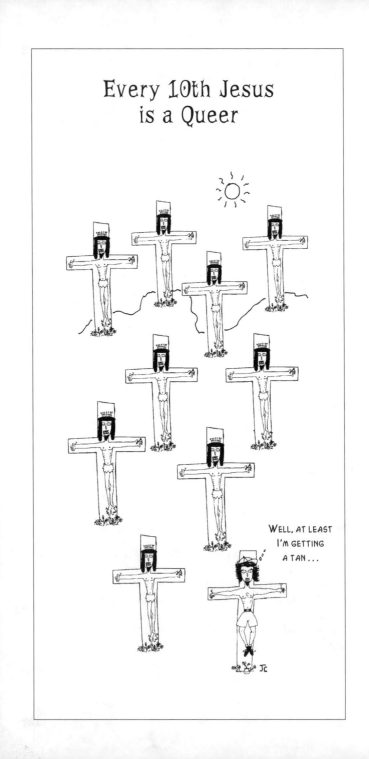

The following is a list of queer or queer-positive religious organizations and churches. They are not all yet freed of the shackles of patriarchy, misogyny, racism or homophobia but most of them are trying pretty damn hard. We applaud their efforts, which is why we have included them here.

The Pope (capitol *P* because he has size issues) recently issued a statement that, at face value, seems to be very supportive of a positive change in the roles of women in the church. Despite his lip service, it is obvious to anyone with two brain cells to rub together that it will still be a cold day in hell before any person with a vagina gets to preside at Holy Eucharist, absolve sins, perform marriages, etc. At least one Episcopal bishop (small *b* because he is more secure with himself) is up to his neck in scalding water. He is on trial for heresy for ordaining an openly gay man (who has a male partner) as a priest. Gay men have been priests since before Thomas Beckett, but now folks are getting tried for heresy for *not* lying. What a lovely message to send to today's youths: *Lie and we'll overlook it.* To all the hypocrisy and blatant bigotry of the dull old patriarchy and its lapdog toties we say: "Get the fuck over yourselves, already."

On New Year's Eve, the First United Lutheran and St. Francis Lutheran Churches (of which Pansy is a member) were expelled from the Evangelical Lutheran Church in Amerikkka (our emphasis) for their refusal to revoke the ordinations of two lesbians and one gay man as pastors. Apparently, at the time, the naughty threesome refused to take vows of celibacy, though their heterosexual counterparts were not required to be chaste. *E.L.C.A., shame, shame, go AWAY, come back again some other day, little fag want to play.*

Despite these continuing obstacles, the increasing recognition of gay men and lesbians by certain officials, churches and congregations seems liberating (can you say "free at last"?). Many churches in San Francisco are no longer just places of worship but homes to programs including PFLAG, various recovery support groups, and altar guilds. If none of this appeals to your spiritual side, then perhaps you should join Betty's religion that features cigarettes, card-playing, anonymous sex and *Melrose Place.* See Cruising for meeting times and locations.

We insist that you phone the numbers listed here to insure proper worship times and locations. If you are a high church queen (the gowns, oh, the gowns) you will not want to be bored to death at some low church worship experience. Be specific about what you are shopping for (like when you pick up a hooker). Pansy finds most of these organizations to be very friendly and open to visitors and newcomers.

If you know of a church that deserves our attention, for good or bad, please drop us a line to that effect, in care of Cleis Press. We will follow up on all good leads.

Affirmation (Church of Jesus Christ of Latter Day Saints)
150 Eureka St. Phone: (415) 641-4554.

All Saints Episcopal Church
1350 Waller. Phone: (415) 621-1862.

Bethany United Methodist Church
1268 Sanchez St. Phone: (415) 647-8393.

Calvary United Methodist Church
1400 Judah St. Phone: (415) 566-3704.

Church of Saint John (Episcopal)
1661 15th St. and Julian. Phone: (415) 861-1436.

Church of the Advent of Christ the King (Episcopal)
261 Fell St. Phone: (415) 431-0454.

Congregation Ahavat Shalom (Jewish)
Phone: (415) 621-1020.

Congregation SH'AR Z'HAV (Jewish Reform)
220 Danvers St. Phone: (415) 861-6932.

Dignity (Roman Catholic)
Phone: (415) 681-2491.

First United Lutheran Church
6555 Geary St. Phone: (415) 751-8108.

Gay/Lesbian Christ Center, Evangelicals Concerned
Phone: (415) 861-0593.

Gays at Newman Hall at UC Berkeley
(Roman Catholic, Paulist)
Phone: (510) 848-7812.

Glide Memorial Church (Methodist)
333 Ellis St., #518. Phone: (415) 771-6300.

Grace Episcopal Cathedral
Taylor and California. Phone: (415) 776-6611.

Integrity (Episcopalian)
Phone: (415) 553-5270.

Lesbians at Newman Hall at UC Berkeley
(Roman Catholic, Paulist)
Phone: (510) 848-7812.

Lutherans Concerned
566 Vallejo St., #25. Phone: (415) 956-2069.

Metropolitan Community Church, Golden Gate
1600 Clay St. Phone: (415) 567-9080.

Metropolitan Community Church, San Francisco
150 Eureka St. Phone: (415) 863-4434.

Most Holy Redeemer Parish (Roman Catholic)
100 Diamond at 18th St. Phone: (415) 863-6259.

Noe Valley Ministry (Presbyterian Church, USA)
1021 Sanchez St. Phone: (415) 282-2317.

Old Saint Mary's Church (Roman Catholic, Paulist)
660 California St. Phone: (415) 986-4388.

Quaker Meeting
(Religious Society of Friends, Pacific Yearly Meeting)
Phone: (415) 431-7440.

St. Aiden's (Episcopal)
101 Goldmine Dr. Phone: (415) 285-9540.

St. Francis Lutheran Church
152 Church St. (how prophetic). Phone: (415) 621-2635.

St. Gregory Nyssen Episcopal Church
500 DeHaro St. Phone: (415) 885-2995.

Trinity Episcopal Church
1668 Bush St. Phone: (415) 775-1117.

Trinity United Methodist Church
48 Belcher St. Phone: (415) 626-0931.

Unity Christ Church
2690 Ocean Ave. at 19th St. Phone: (415) 566-4122.

Church News

What a season of victory this has been for our struggling Church Family!

Under the spiritual direction of Deacon Munger Jones, sister Vera James has recalled her lost years of Satanic possession during her childhood in San Francisco. Last week Munger cast out the demon of lustful appetites and the demon of suicidal urges. Isn't it good to see Vera smiling again? (Her bandages come off next Friday.)

Brother Bob Bickle assumed the leadership of our Teen Boys' Outreach program after ex-Brother Herb Fingers was indicted for molesting our teen boys. (God will forgive Herb. Can we?) We pray that Scooter, Todd and our other lads will soon be back to normal.

Brother Poker Dodds has finished his map of the Holy Land! "Uncle Poke" constructed his model out of 57 cans of colored Play-doh on top of his ping-pong table. The model, which traces the exciting conquest of the Canaanites, is on display in Poker's basement. Poker extends a special invitaion to our troubled Teen Boys in their time of need.

Finally, Mildred Moss has returned from 63 years of service in the Congo, where she ran a Bible School for the natives. Mildred will present her cannibal puppet show "The Savage, My Pupil" this Sunday evening. And hear her spirited performace of Kumbayah on the ukulele. So "come by here" next Sunday for real Christian fun!

Jubilant in His Service,
Pastor Billy Bob Bucketts

Of course you're lovely —
but you still need help.

things not to miss

Despite appearances, liquor and sex are not the only highlights of the San Francisco experience. This chapter provides some delightful tidbits and treasures that we personally feel are not to be missed. If you know of any others, drop us a line for the next edition.

A Different Light Bookstore

489 Castro. Neighborhood: Castro. Map: pg. 160.
Phone: (415) 431-0891. Hours: 10 a.m. to midnight, 7 days a week.

A Different Light Bookstore is the center of the queer universe. If you're queer, have half a brain, and are in San Francisco, you must at least visit. It is cruisy, social, academic, political, entertaining, educational and, by default, the gay community center of San Francisco. What other bookstore can boast that their staff includes published authors, beauty queens, ex-editors of gay rags, singers, lesbian avengers, magazine moguls, ex-monks, performance artists, dancers, porn stars, tattoo artists, vegans, filmmakers, journalists, ivy-league graduates, artists, transgendered folks, art gallery owners, and presidential candidates? The queer book sections include fiction, comics, biography, sexual diversity, politics, recovery, changing men, affirmation, psychology, family issues, bodybuilding, health and fitness, parenting, poetry, essays, travel writing, AIDS (both social/political and treatment/care), grief and dying, queer theory, drama, film and TV, music and dance, mystery, cookbooks, science fiction and fantasy, lesbian non-fiction, lesbian erotica, spirituality, religion, history, children's, youth, young adult, reference, business and law, couples, bisexuality, gender studies, coming out, sexuality, humor, Spanish, German, French, gift books, S/M, body alteration, male erotica, and travel. Besides books, ADL also carries newspapers, magazines, literary journals, 'zines, music, videos, T-shirts, cards, posters and lots of other sideline items. This is the best place in town.

ACT-UP/Golden Gate

519 Castro, Suite 93. Neighborhood: Castro. Map: pg. 160. Phone: (415) 252-9200.

This group meets at Mobilization Against AIDS' office at 584B Castro Street every Tuesday at 7:30 p.m. Committees on treatment issues, HIV prevention, federal issues, state issues, and city budget working group meet regularly. Call the number listed for more information.

Bear Shop

367 9th St. at Harrison. Neighborhood: SOMA. Map: pg. 174.
Phone: (415) 552-1506. Order: (800) 334-3877.
Hours: Mon thru Fri 10:30 a.m. to 6 p.m.

This is the office of Brush Creek Media—the guys who bring you *Bear Magazine*, *Powerplay*, and other bear-loving products. The small shop offers T-shirts, videos, mags, sex toys and other goodies. If you are a bear lover or would like to thank these guys personally for what they do, we suggest you stop in.

Build

483 Guerrero. Neighborhood: Mission. Map: pg. 176.
Hours: Tues thru Sun 12 to 7 p.m.

Build wears many hats as a furniture store, art gallery, and performance and meeting space. They have been host to live jazz bands, film screenings, all-girl lollygags, hootenannies, potluck dinners, and a superswap. Fun, fun. Maybe Betty should see if they will let her have San Francisco's First Annual Spades Tournament here.

Castro Theater

429 Castro at Market. Neighborhood: Castro. Map: pg. 160. Phone: (415) 621-6120.

You simply cannot leave San Francisco without having attended at least one film at the Castro Theater, which was here before homos gentrified the neighborhood, and will be here long after we've moved to new locations. One of the great things about the Castro is the audience reaction to a film. If you want a quiet audience, then don't go here. If you love to boo and hiss at villains, scream out loud when the heroine is dragged off by the monster, or cheer when the hero saves the day, then this is the place. If you are lucky, you will get to hear the Mighty Wurlitzer.

Cruisin' the Castro

Trevor Hailey. Phone: (415) 550-8110.

Trevor will give you a walking tour of the Castro that you won't forget. Starting in 1849 and working up to the present, she provides a concise history of the emergence of the gay community in San Francisco and how the Castro became the center of it all. She will take you up and down the two commercial blocks of Castro Street and point out where much of the history took place and how the neighborhood has changed over the decades. The journey ends at the Names Project, with a tour of the facility. The price is $30.00, which includes brunch at the Café Luna Piena (see Cafés & Restaurants, Queer Favorites, page 69). Tours are available Tuesday thru Saturday, begin at 10 a.m. sharp and finish at approximately 1:30 p.m. Be sure to call for a reservation (the best time to catch her is between 5 and 8 p.m.). Betty and Pansy adore Trevor; she is a permanent fixture of our lovely neighborhood.

Digital Queers

584 Castro #528 / San Francisco, CA 94114. Map: pg. 160.
Phone: (415) 252-6282.

Isn't it nice to know that queers have helped pioneer the techno-boom that is changing the face of communications in the 1990s? Sure it is—until you realize that tons of our political and service organizations lack the basic equipment to function efficiently (much less find their place in cyberspace). Enter Digital Queers. The three-year-old, one-thousand-member (and growing) non-profit group dedicates itself to rounding up computers, printers, modems, hardware, software and other techno stuff, and donating it to queer and HIV-related groups in need. But that's not all. DQ also serves as a cyberlocus for on-line queer and HIV activism. New chapters are forming throughout the U.S., and the organization is enjoying a major co-sexual membership boom. (Some new members are even—gasp!—straight.) Where the religious right practices activism through churches, radio and television, queers are now discovering cyberspace as the perfect locale for world-wide community action—and Digital Queers is helping lead the way.

Gay and Lesbian Historical Society of Northern California

973 Market St., 4th Flr. / P.O. Box 424280 / San Francisco, CA 94142.
Map: pg. 160. Phone: (415) 777-5455

Over ten years old, GLHS is home to a staggering collection of publications, organizational and personal papers, and memorabilia. Here's your chance to take a peep into our collective queer attic—from copies of the *LCE News,* the first gay bar rag in the world, published right here in San Francisco in the early sixties, to the voluminous files of Del Martin and Phyllis Lyon, founders of the Daughters of Bilitis, to the late author Robert Chesley's rough-hewn étagère displaying baby-food bottles filled with pubic hair from countless tricks. The archives are now located in newer and more spacious digs a block from the Powell Street MUNI/BART and are open Saturdays and Sundays from 2 to 5 p.m. Researchers are always welcome, and can call to make appointments for times other than those listed on weekends. GLHS member-ship—which includes a more-or-less quarterly newsletter, program announcements, and the simple joy of knowing you are supporting preservation of queer history—is $30.00 a year; write to the post-office box for information.

Josie's Juice Joint and Cabaret

3583 16th St. at Market. Neighborhood: Castro. Map: pg. 160.
Phone: (415) 861-7933.

By day, this is a vegetarian restaurant and café. At night it is transformed into the hottest queer cabaret this side of the Greenwich Time Line. This place features plays, comedians, musicals, open-mike nights, and the occasional fundraiser. The most recent addition has been *Late Night with Joan Jett Blakk*. This queer presidential candidate has taken time out of her busy campaigning schedule to host this live queer talk show. She generally has three or four guests, and their tal-ents and personalities cover just about everything in the queer world. Joan is a naturally talented interviewer and hostess. Her co-hostess was once your esteemed authoress, Betty. There is always something happening at Josie's, and very often it is excellent. Also see Cafés & Restaurants, Queer Favorites (page 71) for more information.

Leather Tongue Video

714 Valencia at 18th St. Neighborhood: Mission. Map: pg. 176.
Phone: (415) 552-2900.

This is a video rental shop unlike any other. They specialize in rare cult videos, magazines and comics. It is also a hot dyke cruisy spot, on the fringe of the cool mixed coffee-house boho area. Dyke-owned and -operated, everyone here looks like a bike messenger. Visit to check out the videos and comix or to see the staff's new hair-do's.

The Magazine

920 Larkin near Geary. Neighborhood: Polk. Map: pg. 168. Phone: (415) 441-7737. Hours: Mon thru Sat noon to 7 p.m.

This place is a collector's paradise. The staff is efficient and an excellent resource whether you know what you are looking for or not. Seemingly half the size of the old location, it really gets crowded on Saturdays, and the patrons brush against each other as they absentmindedly rifle through some of the most collectible porn (straight and gay) available anywhere. This spot is also great for old movie magazines in excellent condition, photos of the stars, etc. To gain entrance to the chained-off section in the back, you must be known, loved and/or admired by the staff. Pansy has not gained entrance but a certain Juris Doctor we both know (who always seems to turn up in the lurkiest spots) has. The neighborhood is a little scary, which probably accounts for the fact that they have business hours—they could easily do business twenty-four hours a day.

Names Project

AIDS Memorial Quilt, 2362 Market. Map: pg. 160. Office: (415) 863-5511. Workshop: (415) 863-1966.

The AIDS Memorial Quilt has become internationally famous. This is the workshop where everything is coordinated, from sewing panels together to preparing for the next viewing of the quilt in other cities. People are extremely friendly and willing to answer questions. If you would like to see a panel of a loved one, they can find it for you as long as it is not on the road. You can get literature regarding the quilt—number of panels, cities on the tour route, percentage of AIDS deaths the quilt represents, etc. They are always looking for volunteers and have a wish list posted in the window of supplies they need. Just to be in this building with thousands of folded panels filed away and people working on new ones is a powerful experience. This is an important place to visit.

The Pacific Center

2712 Telegraph Ave. / Berkeley, CA 94705. Map: pg. 159. Phone: (510) 548-8283. Switchboard: (510) 841-6224 (includes TTY).

Since 1973, the Pacific Center has been providing services by and for sexual minorities. Their staff and volunteers offer counseling, peer support groups, information, referrals, HIV advocacy, speakers, training and support services. These folks can probably help you find anything to do with queers in the East Bay. The gay men's rap group on Monday night has a reputation as support for those coming out and is one of the only spots for gay guys to meet each other.

Theater Rhinoceros

2926 16th St. at Mission. Neighborhood: Mission. Map: pg. 176.
Phone: (415) 861-5079.

This is the oldest surviving gay and lesbian theater company in the nation. Larger productions are held in the main theater with a seating capacity of approximately 150. Newer, more experimental theater pieces are presented in the studio in the basement, which holds a maximum of 60 people. Find out what's playing and catch a show.

Three Snaps Up Presents

P.O. Box 391411 / San Francisco, CA 94039-1411. Phone (800) 473-8658.

These folks hold many successful, popular, local queer parties and other happenings. They are most famous for starting gay roller-skating every Wednesday in San Mateo. At times this theme has been extended to include roller drag and roller underworld. For information regarding Gay Skate, call (415) 967-5283. They have also hosted queer parties at Raging Waters and Great America. Call or write to get information or to be put on their mailing list.

Under One Roof

2362-B Market near Castro. Neighborhood: Castro. Map: pg. 160.
Phone: (415) 252-8527 or (800) 525-2125.

Under One Roof, The Shop for AIDS Relief, brings together over seventy AIDS agencies in a unique fund-raising effort that has generated more than a million dollars to date. One hundred percent of the profits from every sale directly benefits participating AIDS organizations. The store is staffed almost entirely by volunteers, and overhead costs and services are donated by a number of individuals and corporations. This shop used to be open only during the Christmas season but is now going strong year round.

The 12th Step

Taking Care of yourself

Yes, we can be cruel and bitter queens, but we still have hearts. If we believe in anything, it is taking care of Number One, and so we felt it appropriate to impart some of our brilliant advice to you. In this chapter, you will find information that will make taking care of yourself in San Francisco just a little easier.

SELF-DEFENSE

It is sad to say, but bashers, muggers and run-of-the-mill jerks are out to get us. That is why we recommend that you always carry a really good whistle. Make sure it works and is loud. Also you may want to purchase those loud screaming boxes, pepper spray, tear gas (now legal in California) or a gun (legally acquired, of course). We highly recommend model-mugging and self-defense courses of any and all kinds. Co-ed and women-only self-defense classes are available. Call Community United Against Violence (415-777-5500) for more information about these and other classes of interest.

RECOVERY

We feel sorry for people who aren't alcoholics in San Francisco because there's just so much stuff for clean and sober people here. First, the NA helpline (415-621-8600) and the AA hotline (415-621-1326) are both fabulous, though the Al-Anon answering machine leaves a bit to be desired. They are the first contacts you can use to find your people, and don't be shy to ask them for meetings with lots of fags in leather or lots of dykes over fifty or, especially, meetings for young people, because they'll probably know. There actually is at least one bisexual focus meeting, too. SF is the *home* of special interest twelve-step meetings.

The Meeting Place (so subtly named) is a staple of gay AA/NA and a few other programs. On Market at 15th Street (see map, page 160) there are meetings from the crack of dawn until 10 p.m. For counseling and referrals, call 18th Street Services (415-861-4898) on Church Street—don't ask why (see map, page 160). There's a bazillion half-way houses and stuff, and you can get the inside scoop on them at the Castro Country Club (See Bars, Castro, page 19). They also have a list of all gay twelve-step meetings.

Gay AA/NA meetings in San Francisco are filled with fairly new people. Many people who have been around for a while have straight home groups or go to straight meetings because there's more time there, and some would say, more old-style recovery. Check out a number of meetings because every meeting in SF has a totally different flavor. If you hate the meeting, chat up the people who look like you, and they'll tell you where to show up.

A NOTE ON PROSTITUTION

Hooking in SF is basically the same as in any other city—all the gay rags have masseur/escort/straight-up sex for money ads, and street prostitution takes place in a couple of areas. If you want to call an ad, you probably know what you're doing, so we won't offer any advice. Boys with ads are mostly serious professionals who view their work as, well, *work*. Treat them as pros, and you'll have a good relationship with them.

There are two Ho' Strolls of interest here: the drag queen strip on Larkin between Post and Sutter and the boy strip of Polk Street from about Geary to almost California, with the center of the boys' strip being the corner of Austin/Frank Norris Alley and Polk Street. (See map, page 168.) The boys and the queens both are totally tough; and if you mess with them, you will be *so* sorry, both immediately and karmically. Do yourself a favor and behave.

Both of these Ho' Strolls are pretty dangerous these days, and there are a million cops around; don't get involved in anything stupid. Everyone working has his own rate, and he will tell you straight up what it is after, of course, you bring up the issue of price. Do yourself a favor—be explicit about what you want, and make an agreement about price first.

Two things: these are serious drug areas. If you're from out of town, you probably don't have much experience with crystal meth, and Polk Street is probably *not* the place to get that experience. Safe sex is the order of the day. If you think it's safe just because you're having sex with someone who's twenty, you're a damn fool who shouldn't be allowed to whip it out at all. You owe it to yourself and to your affair-of-the-minute to use a condom. Be aware that bragging about picking up hustlers is generally considered tacky. And please—sex with minors is a *big* karmic and legal no-no.

IMPORTANT PHONE NUMBERS

18th Street Services (substance abuse) 861-4898
A Different Light Bookstore 431-0891
ACT-UP/Golden Gate 252-9200
Adult Children of Alcoholics 442-7998
AIDS & ARC Switchboard 861-7309
AIDS Antibody Test Sites 621-4858
AIDS Emergency Fund 441-6407
AIDS Hotline 863-2437
AIDS Info BBS Worldwide 415-626-1246
AIDS/HIV Nightline 415-668-AIDS
Al-Anon 626-5633
Alcoholics Anonymous 573-6811
Asian AIDS Project 227-0946
Bashing Hotline 1-800-347-HATE
Battered Women Hotline 255-0165
Bay Area Bi Network 564-BABN
Berkeley Free Clinic . . . . 510-644-0425 or 1-800-6-CLINIC
Bi-Pol 775-1990
Black Coalition on AIDS 553-8191
Cancer Information 1-800-422-6237
City Clinic 864-8100
Cocaine Anonymous 821-6155
Codependents Anonymous 905-6331
Community United Against Violence (CUAV) . . . 864-7233
Diamond Youth Shelter 567-1020
Emergency Food Box Program 621-7775
Emergency Shelter 431-2253
Fire Department 911
Gay Legal Referral 621-3900
Gay Rescue Mission 863-4882
Haight-Ashbury Free Clinics 431-1714
Helpline 772-4357
Larkin St. Youth Center 673-0911
Latino AIDS Project 647-5450
Meals on Wheels 495-0333
MUNI 673-6864
Names Project 863-5511
National Hate Crimes Hotline 1-800-347-HATE
Operation Concern (gay mental health services) . 626-7000
Pacific Center (Berkeley) 1-510-548-8283
Paramedics 911

Parents & Friends of Lesbians & Gays (PFLAG) . 921-8850
Police 911
Project Open Hand 771-MEAL
PWA Switchboard 861-7309
SF AIDS Foundation. 1-800-367-AIDS
SF Club for the Deaf. 864-9031
SF Sex Information 621-7300
SF Suicide Prevention/Youth Hotline 752-2000
Shanti. 777-2273
Sisters of Perpetual Indulgence Hotline. 957-3638
STD Testing—City Clinic 864-8100
Suicide Prevention 221-1424
Survivors of Incest Anonymous 566-6226
Taxi Companies
    City Cab 468-7200
    DeSoto Cab 673-1414
    Luxor Cab. 282-4141
    Veteran's Cab 552-1300
    Yellow Cab 626-2345
Time. . . . . POP-ACID
Venereal Disease Hotline 1-800-227-8922
Women's Building (18th at Valencia). 431-1180
Women's Refuge 547-4665

Emotionally Needy
meets
Emotionally Unavailable

Appendices

APPENDIX A:

SAN FRANCISCO QUEER CALENDAR

May 22: Harvey Milk's Birthday. Celebrations often planned.

Last Sunday in May: AIDS Candlelight Memorial and Mobilization. From the Castro to City Hall. Has grown in size every year since it started in 1984. Call (415) 863-4676 for information.

Last Sunday in June: S.F. Freedom Day Parade (Gay Pride Day). Call (415) 864-FREE for information. High Holy Day #1.

First Sunday in August: Dore Alley Fair. This leather-oriented clothing-optional street fair is located between Howard and Folsom and 9th and 10th Streets, SOMA. Call (415) 648-3247 for more info.

Last Sunday in September: Folsom Street Fair. On Folsom between 7th and 11th Streets. Last event of annual leather week. Call (415) 648-3247 for information. High Holy Day #2.

First Sunday in October: Castro Street Fair. Call (415) 467-3354 for more information. High Holy Day #3.

October 31: Halloween is celebrated in the Castro, no matter what day of the week it falls on, and is the most crowded the Castro ever gets. Straight gawkers travel from miles around. The last of the High Holy Days.

November 1 - 2: Day of the Dead. Celebrated in the Mission.

November 27: Milk/Moscone Memorial. Candlelight march from the Castro down Market Street to the City Hall. In 1978, openly gay Supervisor Harvey Milk and Mayor George Moscone were assassinated at City Hall by ex-supervisor Dan White.

APPENDIX B:

TOP TEN PINBALL SPOTS

APPENDIX C:

TOP TEN BILLIARDS SPOTS

APPENDIX D:

CRUISING SPOTS, BY DAY AND NIGHT

See Cruising for more information.

By Day
    A Different Light
    Baker Beach
    Buena Vista Park (south side)
    CALA Foods in the Castro
    The Castro
    Collingwood Park
    Dolores Beach (southwest corner of Dolores Park)
    Golden Gate Park (west end)
    Land's End
    MUNI

By Night
    19th Street (between Church and Diamond)
    Buena Vista Park
    Castro Theater Parking Lot
    Collingwood Park
    Dolores Park
    Dore Alley
    Golden Gate Park (between the windmills)
    Lafayette Park
    Ringold Alley
    Shipley Alley

APPENDIX E:

THE COMMONALITIES OF BETTY & PANSY

We both:

are direct descendants of Mayflower compact signers.

are white trash.

drank Zarex straight from the bottle as children.

have dead aunts named Lottie (Betty's was a dyke).

have fucked people named Wally.

have grandfathers that have allegedly had sex outside their species (a cow and a watermelon).

have grandmothers that are addicts (one mainlines cock tails, the other snorts nutmeg).

have grandmothers who were born on the Ides of March who, strangely enough, are not the ones who are addicts.

have had sex with famous porn stars (and didn't pay), and we won't kiss and tell.

have "little" brothers over six feet tall while we are nowhere close to six feet.

have Lorraines in our lives (Betty's mom and Pansy's sister).

have moms that have been married thrice and annulled once (by the Pope).

have sisters that need to pop out of the closet.

prefer vertical sex.

were named John at birth (surprise)—*John & John's Severe Queer Review* just did not have the same ring to it.

Maps

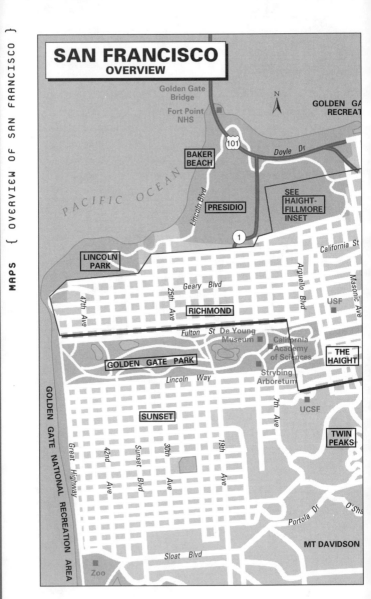

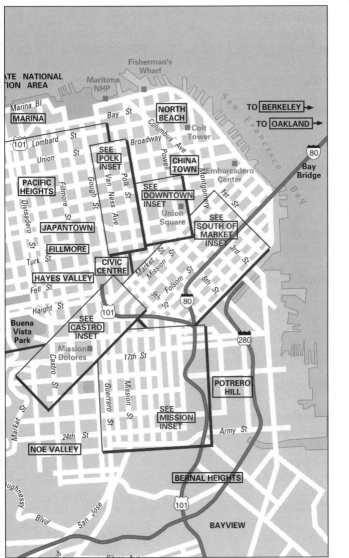

ATE NATIONAL
TION AREA

Fisherman's
Wharf

Maritime
NHP

Marina Bl

MARINA

Bay St

**NORTH
BEACH**

Coit
Tower

TO BERKELEY →

TO OAKLAND →

101 Lombard St

St

Union St

**PACIFIC
HEIGHTS**

Fillmore St

Divisadero St

JAPANTOWN

FILLMORE

Turk St

HAYES VALLEY

Fell St

Haight St

**Buena
Vista
Park**

Gough St

Broadway

Columbus Ave

**SEE
POLK
INSET**

Van Ness Ave

Polk St

**CHINA
TOWN**

Powell

Montgomery

Embarcadero
Center

**SEE
DOWNTOWN
INSET**

Union
Square

San Francisco Bay

80

Bay
Bridge

1st St

**SEE
SOUTH OF
MARKET
INSET**

3rd St

80

101

**CIVIC
CENTRE**

Market St

Mission St

9th St

Folsom St

6th St

**SEE
CASTRO
INSET**

Mission
Dolores

Castro St

280

17th St

Guerrero St

Mission St

**POTRERO
HILL**

**SEE
MISSION
INSET**

Army St

24th St

NOE VALLEY

BERNAL HEIGHTS

101

BAYVIEW

ughnessy

Blvd

San Jose

Silver Ave

Directions to Berkeley and Oakland

BART connects the entire East Bay. The following stations are convenient from SOMA and the Mission (see Maps, pages 174 and 176): the Civic Centre Station, the Powell Street Station, the 16th Street Station on Mission, the 24th Street Station on Mission, and the Montgomery Street Station.

You can also take the Muni at Castro and Market to connect to BART.

By car, take the Bay Bridge. Berkeley is on your left. Oakland is to the right.

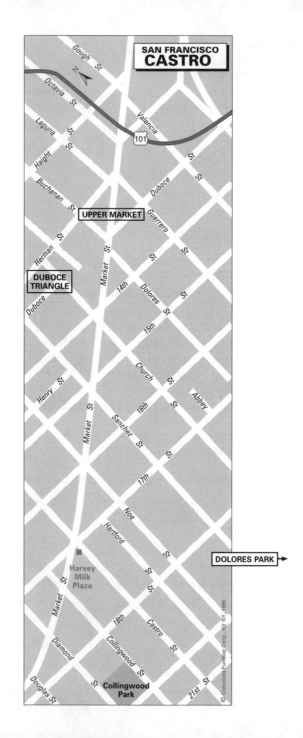

Castro

Castro (cont.)

Duboce Triangle

Upper Market

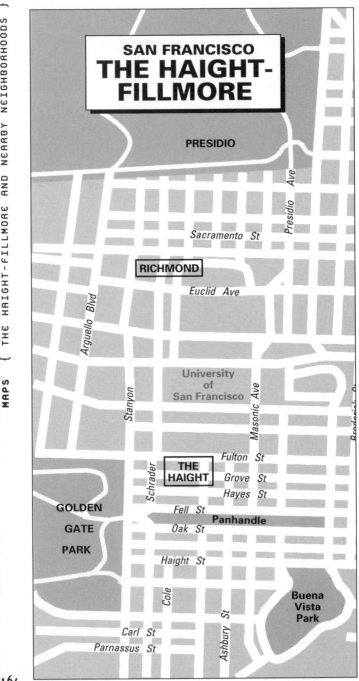

SAN FRANCISCO
THE HAIGHT-FILLMORE

PRESIDIO

Presidio Ave

Sacramento St

RICHMOND

Euclid Ave

Arguello Blvd

University of San Francisco

Stanyon

Masonic Ave

Broderick St

Schrader

Fulton St
Grove St
Hayes St

THE HAIGHT

Fell St
Panhandle
Oak St

GOLDEN

GATE

PARK

Haight St

Cole

Ashbury St

Buena Vista Park

Carl St
Parnassus St

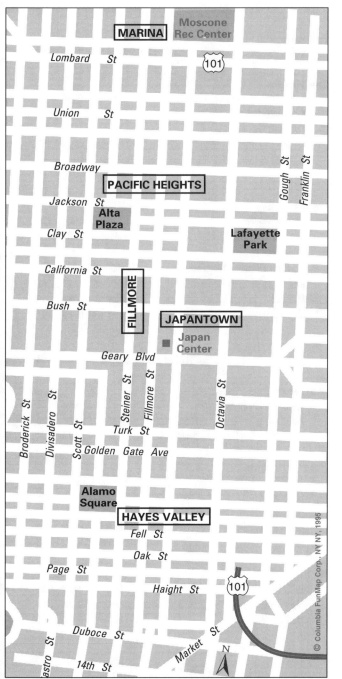

MARINA

Moscone Rec Center

Lombard St

Union St

101

Broadway

PACIFIC HEIGHTS

Jackson St

Alta Plaza

Clay St

Lafayette Park

California St

Bush St

FILLMORE

JAPANTOWN

Japan Center

Geary Blvd

Gough St

Franklin St

Broderick St

Divisadero St

Scott St

Steiner St

Fillmore St

Octavia St

Turk St

Golden Gate Ave

Alamo Square

HAYES VALLEY

Fell St

Oak St

Page St

Haight St

101

Duboce St

Castro St

14th St

Market St

N

© Columbia FunMap Corp., NY NY, 1995

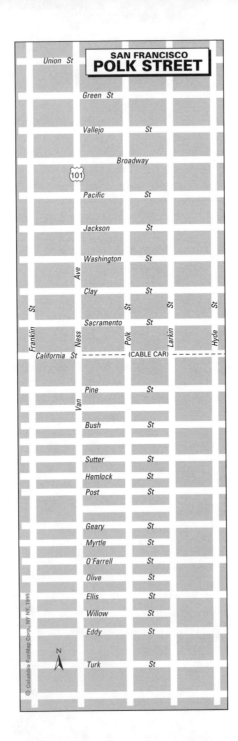

Polk

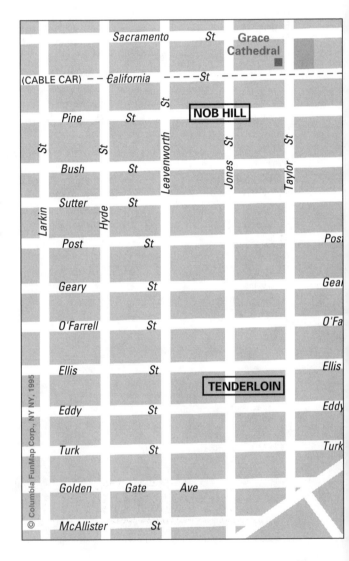

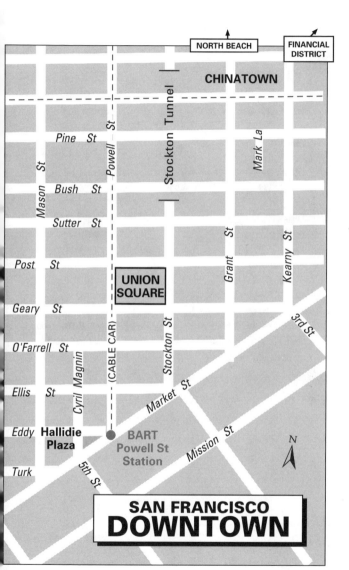

NORTH BEACH

FINANCIAL DISTRICT

CHINATOWN

Stockton Tunnel

Pine St

Powell St

Mark La

Mason St

Bush St

Sutter St

Grant St

Kearny St

Post St

UNION SQUARE

Geary St

O'Farrell St

(CABLE CAR)

Cyril Magnin

Stockton St

3rd St

Ellis St

Market St

Eddy **Hallidie Plaza**

BART **Powell St Station**

Mission St

N

Turk

5th St

SAN FRANCISCO DOWNTOWN

PAGE

© Columbia FunMap Corp NY NY, 1995

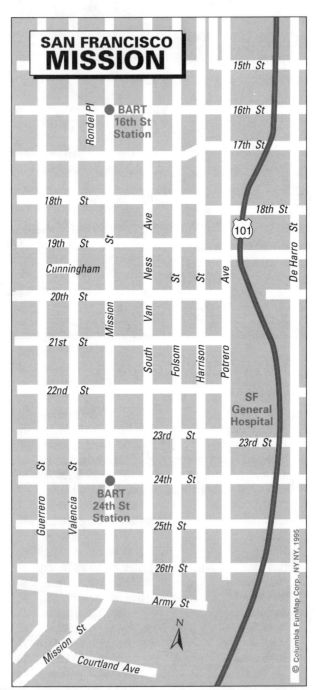

SAN FRANCISCO MISSION

Rondel Pl

BART
16th St
Station

15th St

16th St

17th St

18th St

18th St

Ave

101

De Harro St

19th St

St

Cunningham

Ness

St

St

Ave

20th St

Mission

Van

21st St

South

Folsom

Harrison

Potrero

22nd St

SF
General
Hospital

23rd St

23rd St

24th St

BART
24th St
Station

25th St

Guerrero St

Valencia St

26th St

Army St

N

Mission St

Courtland Ave

© Columbia FunMap Corp., NY NY, 1995

Mission

Indexes

BARS & CLUBS, BY TYPE

OF INTEREST TO WOMEN

GENERAL } INDEXES

About the Authors

Betty Pearl is a well-known dirty scat ho', who spends her days sleeping. She is often found licking her roommate's cat's crusty brownie, and through a happy convergence of needs, giving him a chubbie (the hallmark of consensuality, okay PETA?). When not watching *Melrose Place,* Betty can be found on her knees, asleep, next to a gloryhole at City Entertainment, with a note taped to her head saying, "Wake me when you're ready to stick your dick through the hole."

Pansy, in her own particular refinement on the wonders of the body, enjoys, well, she likes to sniff dirty bung-holes. If given the opportunity and the technology, this chick will throw clods of dirt at the short bus she should be riding. As a sympathy ploy, she will often resort to enacting highly rit-ualized "body memory" scenes. Unfortunately, the only people who respond well to this tend to be men who want to talk about their feelings and practice techniques for flaccid orgasm.

About the Artist

Jim Coughenour is the author of various minimal fictions and the creator of a tasteless line of greeting cards. (Visit his Daimonix Home Page on the Internet). He is currently at work on the novel *Doodler: A Psychomachy in Several Parts.*

Queer Across Canada the U.S. and XXXX, too.

Planning a trip to Canada this summer. Get 100% of the vacation at 70% of the price! Visit Toronto where you'll find North America's largest Gay Pride Celebration at the end of June. Let Columbia FunMaps® lead the way. Our new Montreal/ Quebec and Toronto FunMaps® are available through most gay & lesbian frequented locations or order Travel Paks directly from Columbia FunMaps®.

Choose Any Four FunMaps® for $8.00 or a FunMap® TravelPak of all available maps for only $18.00.

(Check maps from list below. Then copy this page and send it to Columbia FunMap, 118 East 18 Street, New York, NY 10016, or call us at 212-447-7877.)

❑ Atlanta
❑ Chicago
❑ Cincinnati/Columbus/ Dayton
❑ Denver
❑ Fort Lauderdale
❑ Hawaii
❑ Key West
❑ Long Island

❑ Los Angeles
❑ Miami/Miami Beach
❑ Manhattan
❑ Montréal/Quebec City
❑ New Orleans
❑ New York (Upstate)
❑ Northeast Resorts
❑ Palm Springs
❑ Philadelphia/New Jersey

❑ Provincetown/Boston/ Providence
❑ San Diego
❑ San Francisco/Russian River
❑ Seattle
❑ Southern New England
❑ Toronto
❑ Wash, DC/Rehoboth Beach/Baltimore
❑ Wisconsin

❑ Please rush me the maps indicated above.   ❑ Please send me a FunMap TravelPak.

Enclosed please find a check for $_____.

Name _____

Address_____ City_____ State ____ Zip _____

Columbia FunMap®

118 East 28 Street, New York, NY 10016   212-447-7877

Books from Cleis Press

SEXUAL POLITICS

*Body Alchemy: Transsexual
Portraits* by Loren Cameron.
ISBN: 1-57344-063-9 34.94 cloth;
ISBN: 1-57344-062-0 24.95 paper.

*Forbidden Passages: Writings
Banned in Canada*
introductions by Pat Califia
and Janine Fuller.
ISBN: 1-57344-020-5 24.95 cloth;
ISBN: 1-57344-019-1 14.95 paper.

*Good Sex: Real Stories from Real
People*, second edition,
by Julia Hutton.
ISBN: 1-57344-001-9 29.95 cloth;
ISBN: 1-57344-000-0 14.95 paper.

*The Good Vibrations Guide to
Sex: How to Have Safe, Fun Sex
in the '90s* by Cathy Winks and
Anne Semans.
ISBN: 0-939416-83-2 29.95 cloth;
ISBN: 0-939416-84-0 16.95 paper.

*I Am My Own Woman: The
Outlaw Life of Charlotte von
Mahlsdorf*
translated by Jean Hollander.
ISBN: 1-57344-011-6 24.95 cloth;
ISBN: 1-57344-010-8 12.95 paper.

*Madonnarama: Essays on Sex
and Popular Culture*
edited by Lisa Frank and Paul
Smith.
ISBN: 0-939416-72-7 24.95 cloth;
ISBN: 0-939416-71-9 9.95 paper.

*Public Sex: The Culture of
Radical Sex* by Pat Califia.
ISBN: 0-939416-88-3 29.95 cloth;
ISBN: 0-939416-89-1 12.95 paper.

*Sex Work: Writings by Women
in the Sex Industry*
edited by Frédérique Delacoste
and Priscilla Alexander.
ISBN: 0-939416-10-7 24.95 cloth;
ISBN: 0-939416-11-5 16.95 paper.

*Susie Bright's Sexual Reality:
A Virtual Sex World Reader*
by Susie Bright.
ISBN: 0-939416-58-1 24.95 cloth;
ISBN: 0-939416-59-X 9.95 paper.

Susie Bright's Sexwise
by Susie Bright.
ISBN: 1-57344-003-5 24.95 cloth;
ISBN: 1-57344-002-7 10.95 paper.

*Susie Sexpert's Lesbian Sex
World* by Susie Bright.
ISBN: 0-939416-34-4 24.95 cloth;
ISBN: 0-939416-35-2 9.95 paper.

LESBIAN AND GAY
STUDIES

Best Gay Erotica 1996
selected by Scott Heim,
edited by Michael Ford.
ISBN: 1-57344-053-1 24.95 cloth;
ISBN: 1-57344-052-3 12.95 paper.

Best Lesbian Erotica 1996
selected by Heather Lewis,
edited by Tristan Taormino.
ISBN: 1-57344-055-8 24.95 cloth;
ISBN: 1-57344-054-X 12.95 paper.

On the Rails: A Memoir
by Linda Niemann.
ISBN: 1-57344-064-7 14.95 paper.

*The Case of the Good-For-
Nothing Girlfriend*
by Mabel Maney.
ISBN: 0-939416-90-5 24.95 cloth;
ISBN: 0-939416-91-3 10.95 paper.

*The Case of the Not-So-Nice
Nurse* by Mabel Maney.
ISBN: 0-939416-75-1 24.95 cloth;
ISBN: 0-939416-76-X 9.95 paper.

Dagger: On Butch Women
edited by Roxxie, Lily Burana,
Linnea Due.
ISBN: 0-939416-81-6 29.95 cloth;
ISBN: 0-939416-82-4 14.95 paper.

Dark Angels: Lesbian Vampire Stories edited by Pam Keesey.
ISBN: 1-57344-015-9 24.95 cloth;
ISBN 1-7344-014-0 10.95 paper.

Daughters of Darkness: Lesbian Vampire Stories edited by Pam Keesey.
ISBN: 0-939416-77-8 24.95 cloth;
ISBN: 0-939416-78-6 9.95 paper.

Different Daughters: A Book by Mothers of Lesbians, second edition, edited by Louise Rafkin.
ISBN: 1-57344-051-5 24.95 cloth;
ISBN: 1-57344-050-7 12.95 paper.

Different Mothers: Sons & Daughters of Lesbians Talk About Their Lives edited by Louise Rafkin.
ISBN: 0-939416-40-9 24.95 cloth;
ISBN: 0-939416-41-7 9.95 paper.

Dyke Strippers: Lesbian Cartoonists A to Z edited by Roz Warren.
ISBN: 1-57344-009-4 29.95 cloth;
ISBN: 1-57344-008-6 16.95 paper.

Girlfriend Number One: Lesbian Life in the '90s edited by Robin Stevens.
ISBN: 0-939416-79-4 29.95 cloth;
ISBN: 0-939416-8 12.95 paper.

Hothead Paisan: Homicidal Lesbian Terrorist by Diane DiMassa.
ISBN: 0-939416-73-5 14.95 paper.

A Lesbian Love Advisor by Celeste West.
ISBN: 0-939416-27-1 24.95 cloth;
ISBN: 0-939416-26-3 9.95 paper.

More Serious Pleasure: Lesbian Erotic Stories and Poetry edited by the Sheba Collective.
ISBN: 0-939416-48-4 24.95 cloth;
ISBN: 0-939416-47-6 9.95 paper.

Nancy Clue and the Hardly Boys in *A Ghost in the Closet* by Mabel Maney.
ISBN: 1-57344-013-2 24.95 cloth;
ISBN: 1-57344-012-4 10.95 paper.

The Night Audrey's Vibrator Spoke: A Stonewall Riots Collection by Andrea Natalie.
ISBN: 0-939416-64-6 8.95 paper.

Queer and Pleasant Danger: Writing Out My Life by Louise Rafkin.
ISBN: 0-939416-60-3 24.95 cloth;
ISBN: 0-939416-61-1 9.95 paper.

Revenge of Hothead Paisan: Homicidal Lesbian Terrorist by Diane DiMassa.
ISBN: 1-57344-016-7 16.95 paper.

Rubyfruit Mountain: A Stonewall Riots Collection by Andrea Natalie.
ISBN: 0-939416-74-3 9.95 paper.

Serious Pleasure: Lesbian Erotic Stories and Poetry edited by the Sheba Collective.
ISBN: 0-939416-46-8 24.95 cloth;
ISBN: 0-939416-45-X 9.95 paper.

Sons of Darkness: Tales of Men, Blood and Immortality edited by Michael Rowe and Thomas Roche.
ISBN: 1-57344-060-4 24.95 cloth;
ISBN: 1-57344-059-0 12.95 paper.

Switch Hitters: Lesbians Write Gay Male Erotica and Gay Men Write Lesbian Erotica edited by Carol Queen and Lawrence Schimel.
ISBN: 1-57344-022-1 24.95 cloth;
ISBN: 1-57344-021-3 12.95 paper.

Women Who Run With the Werewolves: Tales of Blood, Lust and Metamorphosis edited by Pam Keesey.
ISBN: 1-57344-058-2 24.95 cloth;
ISBN: 1-57344-057-4 12.95 paper.

LATIN AMERICA

Beyond the Border: A New Age in Latin American Women's Fiction edited by Nora Erro-Peralta and Caridad Silva-Núñez.
ISBN: 0-939416-42-5 24.95 cloth;
ISBN: 0-939416-43-3 12.95 paper.

The Little School: Tales of Disappearance and Survival in Argentina by Alicia Partnoy.
ISBN: 0-939416-08-5 21.95 cloth;
ISBN: 0-939416-07-7 9.95 paper.

Revenge of the Apple by Alicia Partnoy.
ISBN: 0-939416-62-X 24.95 cloth;
ISBN: 0-939416-63-8 8.95 paper.

POLITICS OF HEALTH
The Absence of the Dead Is Their Way of Appearing by Mary Winfrey Trautmann.
ISBN: 0-939416-04-2 8.95 paper.

Don't: A Woman's Word by Elly Danica.
ISBN: 0-939416-23-9 21.95 cloth;
ISBN: 0-939416-22-0 8.95 paper

1 in 3: Women with Cancer Confront an Epidemic edited by Judith Brady.
ISBN: 0-939416-50-6 24.95 cloth;
ISBN: 0-939416-49-2 10.95 paper.

Voices in the Night: Women Speaking About Incest edited by Toni A.H. McNaron and Yarrow Morgan.
ISBN: 0-939416-02-6 9.95 paper.

With the Power of Each Breath: A Disabled Women's Anthology edited by Susan Browne, Debra Connors and Nanci Stern.
ISBN: 0-939416-09-3 24.95 cloth;
ISBN: 0-939416-06-9 10.95 paper.

Woman-Centered Pregnancy and Birth by the Federation of Feminist Women's Health Centers.
ISBN: 0-939416-03-4 11.95 paper.

FICTION
Cosmopolis: Urban Stories by Women edited by Ines Rieder.
ISBN: 0-939416-36-0 24.95 cloth;
ISBN: 0-939416-37-9 9.95 paper.

Dirty Weekend: A Novel of Revenge by Helen Zahavi.
ISBN: 0-939416-85-9 10.95 paper.

A Forbidden Passion by Cristina Peri Rossi.
ISBN: 0-939416-64-0 24.95 cloth;
ISBN: 0-939416-68-9 9.95 paper.

Half a Revolution: Contemporary Fiction by Russian Women edited by Masha Gessen.
ISBN 1-57344-007-8 $29.95 cloth;
ISBN 1-57344-006-X $12.95 paper.

In the Garden of Dead Cars by Sybil Claiborne.
ISBN: 0-939416-65-4 24.95 cloth;
ISBN: 0-939416-66-2 9.95 paper.

Memory Mambo by Achy Obejas.
ISBN: 1-57344-018-3 24.95 cloth;
ISBN: 1-57344-017-5 12.95 paper.

Night Train To Mother by Ronit Lentin.
ISBN: 0-939416-29-8 24.95 cloth;
ISBN: 0-939416-28-X 9.95 paper.

The One You Call Sister: New Women's Fiction edited by Paula Martinac.
ISBN: 0-939416-30-1 24.95 cloth;
ISBN: 0-939416031-X 9.95 paper.

Only Lawyers Dancing by Jan McKemmish.
ISBN: 0-939416-70-0 24.95 cloth;
ISBN: 0-939416-69-7 9.95 paper.

Seeing Dell by Carol Guess
ISBN: 1-57344-024-8 24.95 cloth;
ISBN: 1-57344-023-X 12.95 paper.

Unholy Alliances: New Women's Fiction edited by Louise Rafkin.
ISBN: 0-939416-14-X 21.95 cloth;
ISBN: 0-939416-15-8 9.95 paper.

The Wall by Marlen Haushofer.
ISBN: 0-939416-53-0 24.95 cloth;
ISBN: 0-939416-54-9 paper.

We Came All The Way from Cuba So You Could Dress Like This?: Stories by Achy Obejas.
ISBN: 0-939416-92-1 24.95 cloth;
ISBN: 0-939416-93-X 10.95 paper.

REFERENCE

Betty and Pansy's Severe Queer Review of San Francisco by Betty Pearl and Pansy.
ISBN: 1-57344-056-6 10.95 paper.

Food for Life & Other Dish, edited by Lawrence Schimel.
ISBN: 1-57344-061-2 14.95 paper.

Putting Out: The Essential Publishing Resource Guide For Gay and Lesbian Writers, third edition, by Edisol W. Dotson.
ISBN: 0-939416-86-7 29.95 cloth;
ISBN: 0-939416-87-5 12.95 paper.

AUTOBIOGRAPHY, BIOGRAPHY, LETTERS

Peggy Deery: An Irish Family at War by Nell McCafferty.
ISBN: ISBN: 0-939416-38-7 24.95 cloth;
ISBN: 0-939416-39-5 9.95 paper.

The Shape of Red: Insider/Outsider Reflections by Ruth Hubbard and Margaret Randall.
ISBN: 0-939416-19-0 24.95 cloth;
ISBN: 0-939416-18-2 9.95 paper.

Women & Honor: Some Notes on Lying by Adrienne Rich.
ISBN: 0-939416-44-1 3.95 paper.

ANIMAL RIGHTS

And a Deer's Ear, Eagle's Song and Bear's Grace: Relationships Between Animals and Women edited by Theresa Corrigan and Stephanie T. Hoppe.
ISBN: 0-939416-38-7 24.95 cloth;
ISBN: 0-939416-39-5 9.95 paper.

With a Fly's Eye, Whale's Wit and Woman's Heart: Relationships Between Animals and Women edited by Theresa Corrigan and Stephanie T. Hoppe.
ISBN: 0-939416-24-7 24.95 cloth;
ISBN: 0-939416-25-5 9.95 paper.

Since 1980, Cleis Press has published progressive books by women. We welcome your order and will ship your books as quickly as possible.

Individual orders must be prepaid (U.S. dollars only). Please add 15% shipping. PA residents add 6% sales tax.

Mail orders: Cleis Press, PO Box 8933, Pittsburgh PA 15221. MasterCard and Visa orders: include account number, exp. date, and signature.

FAX your credit card order: (412) 937-1567.

or

Phone us Mon-Fri, 9 am - 5 pm EST:
(412) 937-1555 or (800) 780-2279.

ORDER FORM

CLEIS PRESS

QTY.	TITLE	PRICE

Subtotal	
Shipping (add 15%)	
PA residents add 6% sales tax	
TOTAL	

PAYMENT:

☐ MasterCard   ☐ Visa   ☐ Check or Money Order

Account No: _____ Expires: _____

Signature: _____

Daytime Telephone: _____

Name: _____

Address: _____

City, State, Zip: _____